NOTES TO JOHN

JOAN DIDION

NOTES TO JOHN

ALFRED A. KNOPF NEW YORK 2025

A BORZOI BOOK
FIRST HARDCOVER EDITION PUBLISHED BY ALFRED A. KNOPF 2025

Published by Alfred A. Knopf, a division of Penguin Random House LLC,
1745 Broadway, New York, NY 10019.

Knopf, Borzoi Books, and the colophon are registered trademarks of
Penguin Random House LLC.

Library of Congress Control Number: 2024952225
ISBN 978-0-593-80367-7 (hardcover)
ISBN 978-0-593-80368-4 (ebook)

penguinrandomhouse.com | aaknopf.com

Printed in the United States of America
1st Printing

The authorized representative in the EU for product safety and compliance
is Penguin Random House Ireland, Morrison Chambers, 32 Nassau Street,
Dublin D02 YH68, Ireland, https://eu-contact.penguin.ie.

Shortly after Joan Didion died in 2021, a collection of about 150 unnumbered pages was found in a small portable file near her desk. She kept an assortment of things in the file (the doorman's notes from the night in 2003 that her husband, John Gregory Dunne, died; a copy of the speech she gave at her daughter Quintana's wedding; reservation records from the Hotel Bristol in Paris; a list of guests at Christmas parties; computer passwords). The pages make up a sort of journal in which Didion reported on sessions with a psychiatrist, most of them in 2000. The reports are addressed to John. He is the "you" in the manuscript.

The 150 pages seem to have survived only in this one copy, which is now in the Didion/Dunne archive at the New York Public Library. The archive was placed in the library by Didion's heirs, her late brother's children. No restrictions were put on access.

Didion started seeing the psychiatrist, Roger MacKinnon, on November 15, 1999. She had six sessions with him and then began writing the reports to John. They are her thoughts and reflections about the sessions, which separately involved other eminent psychiatrists. The journal ends a little more than a year after therapy began. It includes an account of a session with MacKinnon that John participated in, on June 7, 2000, so one can assume that the reports were not simply for the purpose of bringing him up to speed. He didn't need to be informed about what was discussed that day. He was there.

Some of the subjects in the journal appear in *Blue Nights,* the last book Didion wrote, which was a meditation on her daughter's life. Didion had started seeing MacKinnon because Quintana had told her own psychiatrist that her mother was depressed and should talk to someone. He felt that the mother/daughter relationship was at the core of Quintana's problems, which he was not having much success resolving. He and MacKinnon collaborated. As their therapy sessions went on, MacKinnon led Didion into thoughts about her relationship to her own parents, aging, fear of others, the importance of work.

There is a letter in Didion's computer from March 2001 to an old friend in California in which she describes the recent "rough few years" with Quintana. "Even I have been seeing a psychiatrist," she writes, "which has been an extraordinary experience and has made me a good deal more open than I think I have ever been."

NOTES TO JOHN

29 December 1999

Re not taking Zoloft, I said it made me feel for about an hour after taking it that I'd lost my organizing principle, rather like having a planters' punch before lunch in the tropics. I said I'd tried to think this through, because I knew rationally it couldn't be true, since the PDR said even twice that dose doesn't reach any effect for several hours and peak effect for 3-5 days of steady dosage. I realized that I had a very closely calibrated idea of my physical well being, very fearful of losing control, that my personality was organized around a certain level of mobilization or anxiety.

I then said that I had tried to think through the anxiety I had expressed at our last meeting. I said that although it had been expressed in terms of work (the meeting in Los Angeles etc) I realized when I discussed it with you that it was focused on Quintana.

"Of course it was," he said. We then talked about what my anxieties were re Quintana. Basically they were that she would become depressed to a point of danger. The shoe dropping, the call in the middle of the night, the attempt to take her emotional temperature on every phone call. I said that in some ways this seemed justified and in other ways unfair to her, because she must be feeling our anxiety as we were feeling hers. "I suspect she feels your anxiety very particularly," he said. I said apparently she did. She had not only told us she did but had also mentioned this to Dr. Kass. It was me and not you she wanted to see a psychiatrist. He said he would assume that she read anxiety in both of us, but that something in her and my relationship made her feel mine more acutely, made her lock into mine. "People with certain neurotic patterns lock into each other in a way that people with healthy patterns don't. There's clearly a very powerful dependency that goes both ways between you and her."

He wanted to know how old Quintana was when we got her, the details of the adoption.* We talked at some length about that, and I said I had always been afraid we would lose her. Whalewatching. The hypothetical rattlesnake in the ivy on Franklin Avenue. He said that just as all adoptive children have a deep fear that they will be given away again, all adoptive parents have a deep fear that the child will be taken from them. If you don't deal with these fears at the time you have them, you displace them, fix obsessively on dangers you can control – the snake in the garden – as opposed to the danger you can't control. "Obviously, you didn't deal with this fear at the time. You set it aside. That's your pattern. You move on, you muddle through, you control the situation through your work and your competency. But the fear is still there, and when you discovered this summer that your daughter was in danger you couldn't manage or control, the fear broke through your defenses."

I said I may have been overprotective, but I never thought she saw me that way. In fact she once described me, as a mother, as "a little remote". Dr. MacKinnon: "You don't think she saw your remoteness as a defense? When she uses remoteness herself as a defense? Didn't you just tell me? She never looks back?"

At this point we talked about Quintana and Stephen, Quintana and Dominique.† He asked me if I would object if he discussed certain things that came up in our talks with Dr. Kass, because he felt they could be useful in his talks with Quintana. I said I would encourage him to discuss anything he thought might be helpful.

Returning to the question of why my anxiety was more troublesome to Quintana than yours: "There's something in you – and this long predates her birth – that makes you think you don't deserve good things. I'm sure you thought you were very lucky

* Quintana was adopted in 1966, shortly after she was born.

† Stephen Dunne, John's youngest brother, committed suicide in 1980. He was forty-three. Dominique Dunne, John's niece, was killed by her boyfriend in Los Angeles in 1982. She was twenty-two. Dominique and Quintana had been close.

when you were given Quintana, and I'm also sure you thought you didn't deserve it, that in some way you deserved to lose her. That's an abnormal pattern of thinking, and it's what makes your very natural anxiety in this situation so much more acute than that of, say, your husband. It goes beyond what it is. It goes back to something else. You grew up, for whatever reason, expecting the worst to happen. You don't expect good things to happen. You somehow grew up without the gene for denial."

5 January 2000

Dr. MacKinnon said he hadn't been aware I knew Hilary Califano, he hoped it wasn't upsetting to see her there. I said it wasn't upsetting, but it did raise the question of what two entirely grown women were doing there – two women who live in the world and have their defense systems, for better or worse, pretty fairly in place.

"Most of the time," he said. "But sometimes things happen in our lives that overtake even the most well-constructed defenses."

I said this led into something he had said last week that interested me – that I had early on used my work and competence as a defense against fear of losing Quintana. I said it had occurred to me that my anxieties about work and money – which became very pronounced as the summer wore into fall – were to some extent – (I broke off)

"A symptom," he said. "Very definitely."

"But not entirely a symptom," I said. "Some of my worry was based on real things."

"Of course. The world is changing. Different values become marketable."

"Exactly. But the world has always been changing, and I've always dealt with it. But this summer, for maybe the first time in my life, I began to feel incapable of dealing with it. I thought it was my age. And part of it no doubt was. Yet this anxiety was very, very exaggerated. As far as money goes, we do have a new movie, and there are other possibilities beyond that. And as far as my other work goes, the only real problem is finding time to do it. But I was terrified."

"That was the depression talking."

"Which came out of the situation with Quintana this summer."

6

"Exactly."

I said we had had a troubling weekend in that respect. She had seemed fine, she had a good friend in from out of town who appreciated her situation, we had even joked, when I had to go to the emergency room for an eye infection, about spending every major holiday in the emergency room but this time it wasn't her. Then we got this call on Sunday, about 12:30. I told him about going down to her apartment. "What did she say happened," he asked. I told him. He asked if she had gone to the police. I said no. You had asked her where her precinct was and she said she didn't know. I said that both of us had avoided asking her too many questions, because she seemed too shaky to risk what might be construed as an interrogation.

"You didn't want to seem accusing," he said.

Exactly, I said. We weren't sure, but it occurred to both of us that she had been drinking. Did we smell liquor, he asked. I said I didn't think so but the windows were open. It was hard to tell, she repeated herself but there was no slurring of speech.

"Do you have an alternate scenario," he asked. I said if I had to construct an alternate scenario – and to understand the situation's contradictions I did – it would be that she had left her friends early, gone to a bar, and met someone who ended up hitting her, either in the bar or on the street or in her apartment. "Where was the blood," he asked. I said it was on the floor between the foot of her bed and the bathroom. "Not in the front part of the apartment then," he said. I saw his point.

I then said that one of the things that troubled both you and me about AA – not AA as an idea, but AA in its more unforgiving mode – was that this kind of theatrical failure seemed built into it. It assumes all-or-nothing. You want a drink and give in, you don't just end up with a hangover and a case of the guilts as you would in real life, you end up in the gutter, or in a bar picking somebody up who's going to hit you.

"You're assuming that it's about drinking," he said.

No, I said. I don't think it's about drinking. That's my point.

I said that you and I had talked about this, and wanted to talk to Quintana about it. But there had been a series of obstacles presented. She was busy, or she didn't want to go out two nights in a row, so we couldn't really see her before the weekend, and then I would not be surprised to see further obstacles. Meanwhile, on the phone, she had seemed fine, a blizzard of efficiency – I had even today gotten a check for medical reimbursement with the paperwork all efficiently highlighted, ready for filing. So now I didn't know. Was it going to be productive or counterproductive to bring this up after so many days?

"You're going to have to feel that out, obviously. It's a question of what she expects you to do. Some adult children – and I think this is one of those instances – have the capacity to place their parents in virtually impossible situations. If you confront them, their unconscious mind says you never trust them, why bother, why not do what I want and lie about it. If you don't confront them, the same unconscious mind says this proves you don't love them, don't care about them. It's like little children. You see me playing in the street and you don't even care if I get run over by a car, they say, but if you do run into the street after them, they say you never let them grow up. I would wonder what idea she has of how you and her father express your love for her – does she need you to over-protect her? Does she need you to accuse her, scold her? Is that her only idea of being loved? Children often think this way, but in normal development there comes a point when they move beyond it.

"I know that one of the things Dr. Kass is trying to do with Quintana – and one of the reasons he wanted you to see me – is to break this pattern where she sets you up to react a certain way and you do it.

"So I think you could talk to her in an indirect way. I think you could say you wonder how she thinks you express your love for her. Because if she thinks you express your love by nagging, or accusing, or protecting, you should talk about it, and she should talk to Dr. Kass about it. This is the pattern we suspect is there, and this is the pattern we have to break."

How, I asked, do most children do this? "They grow up." At what point, I asked. How? "Trust. They come to trust that their parents trust them."

12 January 2000

I said that at the end of the hour last week he had said something about trust or lack of trust between mothers and daughters – feeling trusted being the key to separation, to growing up – that I had discounted as not relevant, not meaningful to me.

I said that however it had stuck in my mind, and later that evening or the next day I had remembered a note I had made when I was making notes for my last novel. I would have made the note at some time after my father died – my father's death was part of the impulse behind that particular novel – but that this note had been not about my father but about my mother. I had looked it up, and it was interesting, because it seemed to indicate some distrust or misunderstanding between my mother and me.

I showed him the note. Well, yes, he said. There you are. Extraordinary insight.

Extraordinary or not, I said, it's not much help in just getting on with life. It's even counterproductive, considering that my mother is now 89. It's not as if we're going to resolve anything by confronting this.

It's not so much a question of you and your mother, do you think? Isn't it a question of resolving the way you and your daughter deal with each other? Since we all carry in our minds little pieces of our mothers and fathers, isn't it possible that you may have been replicating some of this pattern with your own daughter?

I said that in fact I had mentioned it to her at dinner the other night. She had been interested in it, but the conversation moved away from the personal into discussion of political attitudes in the 1950s.

Yet it was a good beginning, he said. You could reopen it another time. The more you and she talk to each other, the closer you're going to get to this.

I said that right now we really didn't know where we were with her. She had seemed very open for a period of time after she stopped drinking, but now she seemed closed again, resistant. She had at one time asked me to go to an AA meeting with her for example, and I had gone. We had gone to church and then to the meeting and then met you for lunch and it had been a very good, open day. Then we got into the holidays, and she was busy, and when I asked her recently if I could go to another meeting with her she was resistant. She said it wasn't really a good idea to bring in outsiders. Frankly I didn't even know if she was going herself.

Do you want to know how to make her go? he asked. Go yourself to an Al-Anon meeting. Go more than once. You have to find one with people who match your own intellectual and socio-economic level, but that's not so much of a problem in Manhattan. If she knows you're doing that, she's ninety per cent more likely to go herself. And I think she needs a program. Psychiatry alone isn't going to do it for her.

I said I had a problem with Al-Anon. "Sure, and she has a problem with AA," he said. "And you're going to say she's the alcoholic, you're not. And I'm going to say you're the mother of an alcoholic, and she's not going to stay on the program if she thinks you distrust it. I could even say of course you have a problem with Al-Anon, you have a problem with groups, you don't trust them, you don't know what their agenda is. Does that remind you of your mother at all?"

I said that seemed a stretch, but I would think about it. "I'm going to assign you some homework," he said. "I started out doing traditional Freudian analysis, just listening, then I got dissatisfied with the results, so I incorporated some techniques from the behaviorists. The behaviorists use homework to shortcut the process. Here's your homework. Actually show your daughter that note you showed me. Don't tell her about it, show her, because it's quite a document. Tell her you showed it to me. And if she asked what I said, tell her I asked if your mother's distrust of other people was reflected in your distrust of Al-Anon. See what she says. I think you might be surprised what this opens up."

I said that I would see. "I think what I hear in your voice is exactly what you hear in your daughter's voice when you ask her about AA."

I then said that I also wanted to show him a poem Quintana had written when she was about 6, at the beach. I showed it to him. He was extremely impressed with the way she expressed herself, as if she was "born a writer". I said the loneliness in it had struck me, because you never saw it face to face with her. She had been masking her feelings even then. "She must have had some extraordinary reason to do so." I said you mean the adoption, but there were other things that might have been traumatic to her, notably Juan Carlos's death, about which she would never talk but after which she had dreams of a death figure come to take her "but I will hang on to the fence." I told him about coming to NY with Quintana and Rosie the fall after Juan Carlos died and Rosie going home and Quintana being taken care of by agency day help. And later she mentioned Mrs. So-and-so being mean, and I said why didn't you tell me at the time, and she said "I thought it was your job to work for Mr. Preminger and it was my job to get taken care of by Mrs. So-and-so."

"So in some ways she didn't think of herself as a child," he said. "She saw herself as having real adult responsibilities." I said I supposed so, and I also supposed it was natural, or as natural as natural can be in what was a relatively unusual situation: we were both working at home, she was the only child, there was no question of the adults on one side and the children on the other, we were all together in this.

I said she went to her first meeting, at the William Morris Agency, when she was 3. I told him the denouement. "She was worried about the money," he said. "She was worried about something she couldn't affect, something that was adult business."

I asked if he was saying there had been insufficient separation between her and the problems of our daily lives. I said that this had been something we liked in our family life: we were all three in it together. "Given that situation," he said, "I would venture that she was probably exposed to more than she was prepared to handle. She was a child, you were adults, and yet in some part of her mind she clearly started feeling responsible for you."

19 January 2000

I said that I had in fact done my assigned homework. When Quintana came to dinner Monday night, I said, "after a difficult weekend, which I'll go into later," I had mentioned in the kitchen that I had shown Dr. MacKinnon some notes I had made about my mother, and he had asked me a question I wanted to talk to her about. I had then shown her the notes, and said that Dr. MacKinnon's question was whether I thought that my mother's distrust of groups, of other people's possible agendas, had anything to do with my own resistance to Al-Anon, which had come up previously. I said that at that point you (John) had come into the kitchen, and the conversation digressed somewhat, but then Quintana said: "Wait, I want to get back to what Mom was saying." Surprisingly, when she rephrased my question she had translated it this way: "You mean does your resistance to Al-Anon have anything to do with my resistance to AA?"

"Excellent," Dr. MacKinnon said. "Everybody gets an A on this one. What did you say?"

I said I had said that I supposed that was what I meant, yes. She answered it: she said maybe so, yes. She said she had been resistant to AA lately – she supposed she had a bad taste because of Molly, her sponsor, but she realized that she had been missing it and in fact planned to attend a meeting the next evening.

"So get a new sponsor," Dr. MacKinnon said.

I said that was what you had said, and that we had discussed "sponsors" with Quintana for a minute or two, and then Quintana again brought the conversation back to my original question. What was I really asking, she wanted to know.

I said I supposed I was asking if she thought it could help her if I went to Al-Anon.

Yes, she said, I think it might. I said in that case I would go, and in fact you and I were planning to attend a meeting over the weekend.

This is very positive, Dr. MacKinnon said. Very good. "Let me move on here. You mentioned that your husband became part of the conversation. This brings up something Dr. Kass discussed with me". According to Dr. Kass – "and remember this is my reporting what Dr. Kass thinks Quintana is telling him, so there are several levels of deflection or possible error" – "Quintana has the strong sense that when she deals with you and your husband she is dealing with a single person, that neither of you, particularly you, will take an independent stand, that you defend each other against her."

I said I thought that was the way parents were supposed to present themselves to their children. I also said that, on the contrary, as I had mentioned to him in passing in some other context, I had often felt over the years that I was somehow placed between the two of you, being conciliatory to each of you, keeping you from confrontation.

He said he remembered my saying that, and had in fact mentioned it to Dr. Kass, which had surprised Dr. Kass.

I said this much was true: only once, in my memory, did I get angry with you in front of or to Quintana, and her reaction was so alarmed as to put me off ever doing it again. This was the famous scrambled-egg incident, after which, when I was in the shower with her trying to wash her hair and stop her screaming "I hate him", I said we won't live with him any more, we'll go to Sacramento this morning and I'll figure out what to do from there. Whereupon she started sobbing "you can't, you can't, what will Dad say, what will Dad do, please, I won't go with you, you can't go, etc."

You got it wrong, Dr. MacKinnon said. She didn't want to *lose* him, she just wanted to safely express her anger.

Q: And I didn't let her? I took it into the danger zone? Is this pattern part of why she has trouble expressing anger?

He said Quintana seems to feel that she can't have an independent conversation with either of us, that the other is always there. I said that was the way you and I lived, we were always together. "I think you need to find some time alone with her," he said. "Take a little trip." I said that you had taken such a trip with her several years ago, to Monument Valley, and had found it so rewarding that you had been urging me to do it ever since, but what with her schedule and mine it hadn't worked out. "You have to plan it around her schedule," he said. "Just do it."

I said maybe it would be a good idea if she and I went alone to Lori's* wedding – that the three of us had been planning to go but it did present a fairly imminent natural opportunity for her and me to do it alone. "This is great, take a couple of extra days, let her drive you down to Big Sur, anywhere the two of you feel like, walk on the beach, you'll find yourself talking and it won't seem forced to her, I think you'll find there's a big payoff on this little trip you didn't want to make in the first place." I said you might feel that your absence would be noted by my family. "You and your husband and Quintana have bigger problems right now than what your family might or might not and probably wouldn't think."

I said this had been a hard weekend for you, for me, for her. I explained the Nick† narrative, through the e-mail, the call Thursday, the call Saturday, and then more or less resolution by dinner Monday night.

"It was hardest of all on your husband," he said. "He'd told himself he could trust his brother, he found out he was wrong, he made a mistake and that made him feel terribly, terrible guilty."

* Didion's niece.
† Dominick ("Nick") Dunne was John's older brother. They had a strained, sometimes hostile relationship for many years.

It also made him angry, I said.

"He was angry because he felt guilty. That's a useful thing to remember. Parents of children in emotional trouble tend to feel guilty, hopeless – what did they do wrong, what could they have done differently, where did it all fall apart – and they sometimes show it by getting angry. When people get angry, fly off the handle, they're usually feeling guilty, mad at themselves, they should have known better and so forth."

Obviously, I said. In any case, by the time we had dinner Monday night it was more or less resolved. Everybody had said what he or she had to say, which the three of us don't always do.

"You're becoming a great deal more open. I think as you become more open you find other people are more open around you. You and I talk, you and your husband talk, you and your daughter talk – very often in these situations the whole family ends up being treated by proxy."

I said that this entire experience – since July – had been a big learning experience for both of us. "Of course it has been," he said, "and learning hurts, learning can be very painful, you have to open up things you'd rather forget. If it gets too painful for your husband, either Dr. Kass or I could recommend someone he could talk to the way you and I talk."

I said a friend had mentioned this at dinner Sunday night and you had said what you always say, "I'm a Catholic, we have confession." And she had said "When was the last time you went to confession?" This seemed to amuse Dr. MacKinnon inordinately. He laughed and said he could even recommend a Catholic priest/psychiatrist, a Jesuit, he had trained him, he had a parish in Manhattan and an office on Fifth Avenue and this year he was going to be president of the Lotos Club, so he covered all bases (still laughing), all your husband has to do is say the word. "Once when he was a resident he was doing a demonstration interview with a depressed patient, he was in and out in five minutes, he treated the interview as if he were taking her confession, and it worked. You can imagine the envy of the other residents, he had this magic and they didn't."

I said that sometimes I thought all it took to make both of us feel great was a conversation or a dinner with Quintana when she was up. "That's something else Dr. Kass mentioned," he said. "He said Quintana seems to feel this intense pressure from both of you, united, to come over to the house, have dinner, be there."

I said Dr. Kass had mentioned this to us, and we had since tried not to press Quintana about coming to dinner. To the point that even when 4 of her cousins were coming to dinner Saturday night, I was a little uncomfortable about asking her. And in fact we hadn't asked her. Her cousin had. "She still feels the pressure," he said.

"How can we not want to see her," I said. "We're worried about her. We can only know she's safe if we're in touch with her."

You have to disengage, he said. Don't worry. You're getting there.

2 February 2000

We open with Caneel Bay/St. Barth's amenities. I then say that
we went to an Al-Anon meeting, a parents' group, and found it
troubling. I explained why, the emphasis on self, the "success"
stories. I said that only one thing we heard had resonated with us,
and this was just overheard, on the way out: the woman saying
"I can't work, I can't think, I have no idea whether he's using
or not."

"That's exactly what I'd hoped you would hear," Dr. MacKinnon
said. "That's what you need to get from this. You have to be very
specific about what you want to talk about, about what you need
from the group."

I said the format of this group seemed to preclude actual
conversation. "Then find another group," he said.

I said that what had been more valuable in many ways was
running into Julie. I explained her problem and how she seemed
to have made a decision that brought her out on the other side –
a decision she didn't reach at Hazelden or in other rehabs, didn't
reach through AA. It seemed to be a decision she made on her
own – a realization that she was on a nowhere slide and if she
wanted her life she would have to grab it. I said I thought that was
the decision Quintana would have to reach if she was going to
make it, but I didn't know exactly how you came to that decision.

"It takes an inner strength," he said. "Some people find the
resources inside themselves to pull themselves out."

I asked if he had seen the piece in the Times about work being
done on depression as a Darwinian adaptation, a survival
mechanism – depression, if left unmedicated, eventually tells you
it's time to turn your life around. He had seen the piece, and was
familiar with the theory. "The problem with it," he said, "is that
most of the studies done focus on the failures. Not enough work
has been done on the successes."

I said I had discussed the piece with someone [Kathy Reilly] who was a social worker. She had said that absolutely she agreed that depression could be a motivating agent for people like her and me, "but if you're talking about some addict from Red Hook who has no resources to turn his life around, you better medicate him."

"It depends," he said. He said that for eighteen years he had been in charge of the psychiatric clinic at CPMC, "and you know that neighborhood." He saw every resident's cases, and so "saw a great many more cases than I could have seen in a lifetime of private practice." "These were all hard cases, and yet I was amazed at how frequently we would see someone just seem to take hold, make that decision to be well. They call the decision all kinds of things. They call it being 'born again', or 'finding Christ', or whatever else they call it. But all it seems to be is this decision – God only knows where it comes from, because we sure don't – to grab hold."

I said that repeatedly over the past few years – when Quintana expressed unhappiness or hopelessness about her situation – I had tried to explain that she had to make a decision to be happy. That there was an actual benefit to "putting on a happy face". I said I was encouraged to hear that some of what was said at Hazelden seemed to echo this – the "look good to feel good", the "as if" theory – the point being to act "as if" you believed the slogans, and suddenly you found you did believe. I said that I had told her, as an example of this, that I had thought myself in a dead-end situation in my twenties and had finally come to a conscious decision to change it – in this case to break off a relationship with someone destructive and get on with my life.

Dr. MacKinnon wanted to know what was destructive about the relationship. I explained that the person in question was very smart, and had believed that I was very smart, which at an insecure time in my life had been valuable, but that this person was also very destructive to himself, drank too much, was too depressed to work or even take care of himself, etc.

Dr. MacKinnon asked if he was much older than I was. I said he was older than I was, but not greatly so – I guess eight or nine years. Dr. MacKinnon asked if he were an alcoholic. I said it wasn't a word I used at the time but I supposed he so defined himself, since he later went into rehab and as I understood it hadn't drunk since. I said I didn't actually know because we no longer spoke – we had remained friendly after you and I were married but then he tried to sue me over a character in a novel.

"Was the character based on him," Dr. MacKinnon asked. I said more or less, yes, but basing a character on him wasn't really the problem – the problem was that the "character" did something in the novel that this person had done in real life and didn't want people to know about. Dr. MacKinnon asked what it was. I said that the character had beaten up a woman in circumstances pretty much the same as this person had beaten up a woman I knew. Or so I had believed.

"Did he ever hit you?" Dr. MacKinnon asked.

I said yes.

"Did your parents hit you?"

I said no, they never even spanked me. Once my mother slapped me but it was totally understandable.

"Then wasn't it a pretty worldshaking thing to get hit by this man?"

I said yes, it was, but I had at the time been able to rationalize it, or distance it, as "literary", "real life", an example of romantic degradation.

"Did you blame yourself?"

Definitely not, I said. I blamed him. I blamed him or alcohol or something else, not myself. I said I had naturally asked myself this, since everything you read about domestic abuse is based on the notion that the victim blames herself. I didn't.

"Yet you remained friendly even after you were married?"

I explained that we were all friends, that you and I had in fact met through this person.

"Your husband didn't resent this friendship?"

Why should he have, I said.

"Most people are possessive about the people they're married to. Wouldn't you resent having an old girlfriend of his around?"

No, I said. In fact an old girlfriend of yours had been over the years – although we rarely saw her, because she lived in England – one of our best friends. I had even once called her (she worked for BA) to get Quintana onto a flight from Nice to Heathrow.

"You really don't know what I'm talking about, do you?"

No, I said. What are you talking about?

"It's as if you operate on a different level. Maybe it's the entertainment industry."

"If you mean many people I know get married a lot of times and stay on good terms with their ex-wives and husbands, that's true."

"Only a very small percentage of people do that. In the rest of the world, people regard their wives or husbands possessively."

"I think they're unhealthy."

I said, in a conciliatory way, that in fact your parents had been married only once, my parents had been married only once, my brother has been married for 40 years, and you and I were married 36 last Sunday. So we were not entirely operating on entertainment-industry rules.

"You mentioned a few weeks ago that your father had been depressed."

I said yes, he was. I said I had looked a few weeks ago at the letters he had left in his safe deposit box for me and my mother. My mother had given them to me just after he died, saying that she could not bear to read hers, "so you take it". There had also been one for my brother but I never saw it. At the time I was given the letters, right after he died, I read them once and then put them in a box – I didn't want to dwell on them. A few weeks ago, when I took them out of the box and read them again, I noticed something – I hadn't noticed it before – that shocked me. The letter to Mother was dated 1953, and the letter to me 1955. The letter to me began by saying that certain things were happening that suggested he wouldn't be around much longer, and the letter to mother didn't say but implied the same thing.

"Do you think he had just gotten bad news about his health?"

I said if he had just gotten bad news about his health, it was seriously off the mark, since he lived forty more years.

"Then what shocked you?"

I said they read almost like suicide notes.

"Goodbye notes. Yes. That's certainly what they sound like. Obviously you must have had some idea of his state of mind at the time."

I said I had known of course that he was depressed. He was in and out of Letterman. He could only eat raw oysters. Mother would drive down from Sacramento on Sundays and pick me up in Berkeley and we would go over to San Francisco to see him. We would pick him up at the hospital and drive somewhere – anywhere – then go somewhere to eat oysters. Then he would want to be left off as far from the hospital as possible. The hospital was in the Presidio. Do you know San Francisco, I asked.

"I was stationed at the Naval Hospital in Oakland during the same years you're talking about," he said. "So yes. I know the hospital you're talking about."

All right, I said. Where he wanted to be let off was always on the beach to the south of Golden Gate Park.

"People die there," Dr. MacKinnon said. "Heavy surf, heavy rip tide. That must have gone through your mind when you dropped him there, knowing how depressed he was."

I said I didn't remember thinking this. I just thought how sad he looked waving goodbye.

"People who are depressed to the point of suicide say little things to people who are close to them – little insignificant things – that may not register in the conscious mind but certainly register somewhere. They end a discussion by saying 'Of course that won't matter to me', things of that nature."

"Are you saying I knew at some level that he was suicidal?"

"I don't see how you could have escaped it. And I don't see how that old unarticulated knowledge could escape coming back into play now – when you're experiencing fears about your daughter."

9 February 2000

Dr. MacKinnon asked how I had felt this week. I said that as he knew, our conversation last week about suicide had disturbed me, but on balance I thought that in the current situation it was useful to me to consider things I had previously, with some success, left unexamined. "That's pretty much the point," he said. I said that in the early seventies I had made several attempts to write a book called "Fairy Tales", the point of which was to look at certain California myths in terms of my family. I had been unable on every attempt to get past about page 30. The problem, I had thought then and still think, was that I was incapable of examining my family – I could have written easily enough about California, but the point here was to look at California mythology as it intersected with my family's mythology, and I had been finally incapable of doing that.

"You mean you would have had to look at some of the ways you might have revised your personal history," he said. "That would have been too painful?"

I said I never got as far as thinking that. I had just moved on, moved away from it, moved past it. I said this was in fact the very strategy I had taken from all those pioneer California stories. The crossing the plains story, the burying your child on the trail story. "In the case of the pioneers it was a question of survival," he said. I said I supposed that this was too. "Well, yes," he said. "A different kind of survival."

"And now," he suggested, "you're in a situation where your survival strategy isn't working so successfully."

I said that obviously I couldn't move on or past Quintana, so right, the strategy wasn't working. I said I had been wondering about his remark that Dr. Kass thought Quintana was making good progress. I said that to some extent we thought we too saw progress. I told him about dinner Friday night at the Four Seasons, during which she had seemed – to both you and me –

a little distant, or remote, or guarded. You had remarked on this after dinner, saying that although this might be painful for us, this distancing was definitely where she needed to go.

"It is," he said. "Exactly. But you didn't feel it that way?"

I said that I had felt as you had, but our positive construction on this had been pretty thoroughly dashed by a phone call from her late Saturday afternoon. The ostensible subject of the call was a letter she had gotten from a childhood friend – the older sister of the childhood friend who had died on heroin – saying that she herself, the older sister, had attempted suicide. I said that Quintana seemed to have been drinking. There were repetitions, there was some slurred speech. We had tried to keep her on the phone, asking about her day, and then we got into a repeated diatribe against technical support lines and the internet and her cell phone and modern life in general, during the course of which she asked if she could borrow my cell phone. I said of course. She said she would send a messenger for it Monday. I said it would be good to clear up her internet problem over the weekend, we could leave it with her doorman on the way downtown.

"Leave it with her doorman? You didn't think of going up?"

I said my instinct at the time was that she would reject a visit. I didn't want to leave her space to say she didn't really need my cell phone.

"You thought she wouldn't want you to see her?"

I said I guessed so.

"You must have had some idea in your mind what it was she wouldn't want you to see? What it was you would see if you went up?"

I said my idea was that we would see some variation on what we saw last summer. That we would find her unsteady on her feet, not making sense.

"The apartment in disarray? Bottles around?"

I said that I was quite sure she would put away any bottles if she knew we were coming. And as far as disarray went, even at the most florid stage of this, the apartment was immaculate. She was almost compulsive about it.

"I wonder if Dr. Kass is aware she's drinking," he said.

I said I didn't know. Given her history, he would of course be alert to the cues. If we picked them up, he could surely pick them up. But when she was pulled together, she was very pulled together. This was part of what made us wonder what he meant by making good progress.

"It's sometimes very hard to tell. I don't treat addicted patients, and this is the reason. The doctor has to have an investment in making the patient better. When you're dealing with an addicted patient, this investment can work against picking up what might be obvious to someone else. You can't ask them direct questions, they react defensively. They interpret almost any question as an accusation. They don't trust other people. They only trust the substance, which they can control. Because they don't trust other people, they're extremely deceptive. They think they have to be."

I said that the element of concealment was maybe what upset me most. I often find myself wishing we could go back to before Hazelden, before the whole problem got named and medicalized and she started thinking she had to hide it.

"She'd been doing a pretty good job of hiding it before that, hadn't she?"

I said I supposed this was true. Of course. I just wished.

"It might be helpful if I were to mention this to Dr. Kass," he said. "I don't think you should talk to him, but there are ways and ways to mention things, impart information that could be valuable in treatment."

I said I thought it could be a bad idea, it could boomerang, it frightened me.

"Because she's so fragile," he said.

Exactly, I said. And Dr. Kass seems at the moment one of her few lifelines. If she were to think he was confronting her in any way, she could pull away, stop seeing him.

"He would never confront her."

Or, I said, he might pull away from her, decide that she was untreatable.

"I don't think that," he said.

"I can't risk it," I said.

"I won't say anything," he said, "but think about it. If you decide it might be a good idea – I think it would be, but it's obviously up to you – just let me know."

I said I would let him know if I changed my mind.

"Then it was a hard weekend," he said. I said yes. I explained about the busy signals and our relief at getting a ring on Sunday. And then leaving a message and not getting a callback until Monday morning. At which point you admitted you had been thinking maybe whoever murdered her put the phone back on the hook. "But you didn't think somebody had murdered her," he said. No, I said. I thought she had killed herself. Especially since the content of the Saturday call was somebody else's suicide attempt.

"You and your husband are going through hell," he said. "There's nothing you can do right in your own eyes. You go up to her apartment to give her the cell phone, you're intruding on her space. You don't go up, you're abandoning her. You don't even know which she thinks. You can only love her. You can't save her. She came to you with a whole set of genetic possibilities, possibly negative, you can't control. Substance abuse and depression go together, and depression has a genetic component. Environment is a lot, but it's not everything."

I said I couldn't believe that. I myself had come into life with a whole set of what might be called negative genetic possibilities – vide the conversation we had last week – and I had moved away from them.

"It took a lot of work for you to overcome those possibilities, get where you are. Nothing you've told me about your life reads easy, even when you say it was, I suspect your daughter will need to put in the same kind of work."

I said that was what truly broke our heart. To see how hard she was trying. We had tried to make her life easy and we hadn't. I don't mean "easy" in the obvious sense of good houses, good schools, etc. I mean easy in the sense that she would be free of both her own and our history. This seems to be one of the key promises you make when you adopt a child: you will take the child away from his or her history.

"I know," he said. "I have an adopted granddaughter. She's six. I keep forgetting she's adopted. She's just one of us. It would be very upsetting to me if her history turned up to tear that us-ness. That's part of the pain you're experiencing. She already knows you love her, I think all you can do now is believe in her. Believe she'll get better. Trust her. Save your natural mistrust for me. You have to trust she can get better even when the evidence suggests otherwise. Don't focus on the evidence. This is the basic Twelve-Step message. This is what they call 'higher power' or whatever they call it. This is all it is."

"The Hazelden 'as if' message," I said.

"That's all they're saying."

16 February 2000

I said I wasn't sure where we left off. Dr. MacKinnon said why
not begin where you are now. I said I wasn't sure where I was
now, life seemed rather scattered, we had not seen Quintana but
had talked to her, she had seemed on the occasions we spoke
in generally good spirits, fairly upbeat. Still, I found myself
worrying, waiting for the bad news to kick in. I had thought
about what he had said last week – that I had to have faith,
believe that everything was going to turn out – but that I had
difficulty doing this, and I wondered if my anticipating the worst
was in some way transmitting itself to her, worrying her to the
point where it became a self-fulfilling prophecy.

"I think you have to examine how far back in your life you've
been anticipating the worst. Because the farther back this pattern
goes, the more likely it is that she's been picking up on it for a
very long time."

I said I knew that it went very far back, to early childhood. For
example, I keep hearing that small girls imagine themselves as
brides, princesses in wedding dresses. I never had: my earliest
picture of myself being "married" was myself getting a divorce,
leaving a courthouse in a South American city wearing dark
glasses and getting my picture taken.

"You don't think that's unusual? I've never encountered a
childhood divorce fantasy."

I said yes, I did think it was unusual, that was why I had
mentioned it. On the other hand, it reflected nothing in my actual
experience – nobody we even knew at that stage was divorced – it
reflected my reading a lot of trash fiction as a very young child.

"Why were you reading trash fiction? You would have been a
bright child, didn't you go to the library?" I said I was too little
to go to the library by myself. There was a children's library near
our house and my mother would take me there. But I didn't like

children's books, they bored me. "And your mother didn't realize how precocious you were, that you weren't being challenged?" I said I was pretty sure she had realized it, but she might not have wanted to encourage it. "She didn't want to expose you to things you might not have been able to handle?" I said maybe something like that, I didn't know. In any case. The war came and we left and there was no question of libraries until after we came home.

I said that my reaction to the war was another case of having been in retrospect overly apprehensive. "Can you expand on that reaction?" I said in some ways it (the war) began for me when my brother was born, in December 1939. My mother was in the hospital for two weeks. The hospital did not allow visits from children. I felt quite alone, left out. "Abandoned," he said. In a way, I said. Then she came home, and everything was a little different, and I didn't react well. My father and I had been very close – I spent a lot of those first five years just driving around with him, visiting relatives or dropping by ranches or whatever – and after my brother was born this dynamic changed. Plus, the war was always on the horizon. I would hear Daddy talking about enlisting. Which he did, before war was declared. When he went away I was sad for a long time, I stopped growing, the pediatrician called it "failure to thrive" and recommended to Mother that we join him if possible. It was possible, he was only at Fort Lewis then, so we did. Then we went to Durham, then to Colorado Springs.

These were for a child disordered times. There was always difficulty getting trains. I remember there were no seats on the train between New Orleans and Durham, we stood up in the vestibule where the cars coupled. There was always difficulty finding somewhere to live. The first and one of the few times I ever saw my mother cry was coming out of a military housing office in either Tacoma or Durham. In Durham my father was billeted at Duke, and Mother and my brother and I lived in one room in a Baptist preacher's house, with kitchen privileges. This family was strange to me, exotic. The children sat under the back stoop eating dirt, I later learned it was common in poor areas of the south, the result of a nutritional deficiency.

"But your father was getting a salary, why did you live that way?" I pointed out that this was 1942. Every place the military was stationed was overcrowded. It wasn't a question of money. It was a question of no place to live.

"You must have been afraid your father would be sent overseas, maybe die." I said I was. He talked about going overseas all the time. He seemed ashamed that he kept getting orders for one after another office job in safe places. This feeling on his part seemed especially acute in Colorado Springs, because this was a base on which other people were actually in harm's way – fliers from Petersen were always crashing, but he wasn't a flier.

When he left Petersen for Cleveland and Detroit we went home. Except we didn't have a house any more, they had sold it. So my mother and brother and I lived with my grandmother until the war ended and Daddy came home, at which point they built a house, but finding the property and getting the house built took probably another year of living with my grandmother. That was a difficult time for Daddy. During the time he was away, Mother had seemed to work out a very contented life with her mother. "Was your grandfather dead?" No, I said, but he was away from Sunday afternoon until Friday night. She lived in Sacramento, he worked in Marysville. That was their M.O. So it was really a house of women, until Daddy came home.

"There must have been tension. You must have felt it." I said there had been tension, that in fact I had later learned from Mother that it was a period when they considered divorce.

"There has to have been a level at which you knew that. Witness your divorce fantasy."

I said there might or might not have been a level at which I knew it, but in point of fact the divorce fantasy was much earlier, before the war.

"I'm suggesting that the tension may not have arrived out of nowhere in 1945. That you felt it much earlier, even before the war. Sensitive children are extraordinarily attuned to domestic tension, things they hear at the dinner table."

I said I supposed that all children were so attuned. And they had no way of interpreting what they picked up. They had no way of understanding the normal give and take of adult relationships, normal differences of opinion.

"Children have different ways of handling this. Some children close it off, refuse to hear it, don't remember it later." I said that my brother remembered nothing about our childhood. I could not engage him in a conversation about his life before college if our lives depended on it. Of course he was only four, but his entire memory of Colorado Springs is a dead certainty that we left because he saw a spider in a packing box.

"That's something like believing the tension in your household began when the war ended."

I said nothing.

"I think you grew up believing that you were on the brink of disaster. That you were about to lose your father. I think you were anticipating the loss of your father your entire life. Until he died. Which is why I think you took his death harder than you thought you did."

Let's for the sake of argument, I said, assume that this is true. It's certainly true that I have always been extremely apprehensive. The reasons for my being apprehensive may not be as important as the simple fact that I have been. Here's what I don't understand: what has this got to do with Quintana? What is she getting from me that troubles her? I accept that she's getting something, that's what she tells Dr. Kass, that's why I'm talking to you.

"A very simple message. She gets that you're worried, apprehensive, maybe afraid. Children who sense that a parent is always worried feel insecure, from a very young age. They have no idea what the parent is worried about, so they anticipate the worst outcome they can imagine. They're afraid the parent may lose control of the situation, may not be able to take care of them. They carry that fear into adult life. That's what she's working on with Dr. Kass. But she needs to feel that you'll be all right."

1 March 2000

I said that I had been sorry not to see him last week, and in an odd way you had too. We had both been concerned about what seemed a lost ability to make easy contact with Quintana, and you had wondered whether both she and we were down to playing chicken with each other.

Meaning what, he asked.

I said meaning all of us playing out "distance" roles with inadequate regard for possible danger.

You think she's in danger, he said.

I said we didn't know. Some things concerned us. Her failure to call back Susanna* for example. I explained her relationship with Susanna, that it had always been a relationship that didn't threaten her. And yet she was not returning her calls.

Obviously, he said, you must have certain reliable criteria for deciding when she's in danger and when she simply wants to be alone.

I said we had always thought we did have reliable criteria. But the events of the past year had illustrated to us in a dramatic way that the criteria had been wrong. At the simplest level, there had been events that we had interpreted one way and then we had learned in the course of her various hospitalizations that she had seen the events quite differently. Each time she was hospitalized, for example, we heard more about how crucial and disastrous her trip to Hong Kong had been in her eyes. Whereas we had seen it as a positive experience in overcoming jet lag and culture shock. So now we didn't trust our criteria.

And so if she forgets not to sneeze in front of you, he said, you're asking her if she's all right.

* Susanna Moore is a writer who was friends with the Didion/Dunnes in Los Angeles and later in New York.

35

I suppose so, I said. And pressing remedies on her. And then not calling her. We are having dinner with her Friday night – it's her birthday – but it has reached a point where we were even afraid to ask her to dinner on her birthday.

There's a big difference, he said, between saying you expect her for dinner every week – playing on her guilt feelings – and saying we're here if you want to come over, the house is open, we'll tell you if we have something else planned.

I said I always thought that was the way we had put it. But then we found out she didn't see it that way, that she in fact had guilt feelings. I didn't know where they came from. Maybe they were the kind of guilt feelings I had about my parents, maybe they came from nowhere, maybe they were only in her mind.

Don't you suppose, he said, that this is part of what she and Dr. Kass are working on?

I said I supposed so.

Sometimes, he said, a child will say, in one breath, she's always pressuring me to come over, she won't let me alone. And, in the next breath, she doesn't care about me, she never calls, I'm alone and she doesn't care.

I think that's where we are, I said.

I think you are too, he said.

Which is not to say I think she's manipulative, I said. I don't. She's never been manipulative.

What you're saying is that she doesn't try to be. Quite clearly, she's manipulating you and her father to the point where you don't know which way to turn.

I said I thought that in some ways this whole period had been harder on you than on me. I said you dealt with things fairly directly, and nothing about this was direct.

You may have the advantage of having someone to talk to about it.

I said that you and I talked at length about what he said.

That's fine, he said, but from your husband's point of view it's secondhand, it's passive, his own feelings don't come into play.

Change of subject. I said that when I saw him two weeks ago, and we were talking about World War II, he had said something about how mothers during World War II had done an extraordinary job of protecting their children from the fear of losing their families, had drawn on extraordinary resources to allow their children to grow up unparalyzed by fear. I said I had thought about this, and wondered whether he had been suggesting that my own mother had not been able to so protect me – or that I had believed her unable.

I was raising the question, yes, he said. I don't know the answer. Obviously, it was something I wanted you to think about.

I don't know the answer either, I said. I do not remember ever thinking my mother incapable of protecting me. The only time in my memory I ever felt, as a child, absent her protection was once during the war when we were driving across the country to Sacramento. I was probably eight, my brother three. I woke up. It was dark. He and I were in the car, and Mother and Daddy were gone. The car was parked on a residential street, I didn't know where but I figured it was Reno because that had been the next town on the map when I fell asleep. I remember assuming that something overwhelmingly urgent had happened, and that they would not be coming back for us. I figured out what to do: my mother had left her mink coat over us, and as soon as it was light I would take my brother and the coat and walk downtown. We would sell the coat for enough money to get a bus to Sacramento. The main problem would be explaining it to my brother in a way so as to enlist his cooperation rather than his panic.

That would have been very frightening, he said.

I said I didn't remember being frightened. I remembered being galvanized, ready to do what I had to do.

Then you must have been left alone a lot.

Probably never, I said. If I'd been left alone a lot, I wouldn't have immediately assumed this was something overwhelmingly urgent, would I?

Did you talk to your mother and father about this when they came back to the car?

I was asleep when they came back.

The next day? Did you mention it then?

No. We got to Sacramento. It was wartime. Things happened.

I was reading John McCain's book, he said. It gives a very interesting sense of growing up in the military, moving from place to place.

Did it bother him, I asked.

Very much, he said. How could it have not bothered him? Adolescents who get moved around tend to express their anger and loss, but younger children don't. They internalize it. They grow up expecting always to be the new kid in school, the outsider. It interferes with their socialization. To one extent or another, they grow up inadequately socialized.

I said we had moved Quintana around a good deal as a small child. Not actually "moved" her, just taken her with us into various working situations for various lengths of time in other places. I mentioned Nick saying "she's remarkably well adjusted, considering that every time I see her she's in a different city." I mentioned bringing her back to nursery school just in time for the Christmas pageant and of course she had missed learning the carols. She had always seemed amenable to these sudden moves, but maybe it had to some extent interfered with her socialization.

She had seemed later to always feel herself an outsider, the odd child out among her peers.

I fell silent. He asked if I were sad or depressed.

I said not.

Tired then?

A little tired, I said, and a little distracted. I said I was working on a movie with a lot of plot. Trying to keep all the threads in mind. Sometimes I forget the threads. So many threads that sometimes I worried I was in the beginning stage of Alzheimer's.

Is that something you fear?

Doesn't everybody?

Some people fear it more than others. Depending on their family histories.

I said that the three of my four grandparents who had lived long enough to have it didn't. My mother, at 89, had residual brain damage from a subdural hematoma and surgery, but no dementia whatsoever. My father had shown signs of dementia, as early as 1984, when he forgot which of two hospitals he had dropped my mother at an hour before, but on the other hand my father had drunk a great deal, especially during the last 30 years of his life. And by the time he died in the early 1990s, his confusion hadn't really gotten a whole lot worse than it was in 1984. So I didn't think I had reason to be deeply afraid of Alzheimer's. I was just distracted.

Sometimes it's hard to think about these things when you're worried about work, he said.

I think that's my situation today, I said.

8 March 2000

I said that I had typed up something I wanted to show him.
I had found notes I had taken after 2 interviews with the UC
psychologist I saw in 1955. One set of notes was on a torn-out
notebook page, the other partly typed with handwritten notes
added. Reading them, I said, I had been struck by how they
seemed to address the very things we were talking about, and
discouraged by how little progress I had made toward addressing
these things during the 45 intervening years.

He read the notes, which were made in January and March 1955.
(attached). "She was really very good, she got right to it," he
said. "Why did you only see her twice?" I said I hadn't only seen
her twice, I had seen her for at least an entire semester, maybe
longer, that was part of the deal, seeing her was what I had to do
to move out of the Tri Delt house. One set of notes had to do with
my feeling myself an outsider. "The war years, moving around,
very common," he said. "Some children who are very secure in
themselves perceive those moves differently – they see a whole
new world opening up with every move. Clearly, you didn't."

The second set of notes had to do with my apprehension about
my father dying. This was 1955, the same year my father wrote the
goodbye letter to me that was still in the safe deposit box when he
died. "So some fear of what might happen to him seems to have
been coming through to me at the time," I said. "Of course it
was," he said. "We know that, we talked about that."

Why couldn't I see it at the time, I asked. Why did I forget all this
in between. "You couldn't afford to see it at the time. You were at
a stage in your life when you wanted to be free. The whole reason
you were talking to this woman was because you had made a
step toward freedom. Naturally, you would have resisted her.
You would have felt that seeing a psychologist was a constriction
placed on you, a way of keeping you dependent. You want
freedom, they were telling you, you must need help, you must be
sick."

40

I said I had read a poem this week I couldn't seem to shake, and thinking about why made me realize something. The poet, Rosanna Warren, was addressing the reader. The conceit is that the reader, "Lilly", is looking at a triptych of life. "You want to buy that center panel, Lilly, but you can't have that alone," the poem goes, and then later: "No, you can't buy the central panel alone, with the king and queen / joyous and powerful in their open boat, the baby bespeaking freedom / and the net full of fish flashing in blessed abundance. . . ." And then: "because the oarsman is blindfolded / because the crowned fisherman has his back to us / because that open boat / has not set sail / from our shores / nor will it, while we are alive."

"You still want the center panel," he said.

"Exactly," I said. "I still want to see myself as the mother in the open boat. Joyous and powerful. I don't want the oarsman, the oarsman is Charon. I don't want the fisherman to turn to me, the fisherman is Christ. The end of the poem is death. I realized that maybe part of where I am now is that I never made myself ready – somehow failed to prepare myself – for how old I am, where I am now in life. And I began wondering if it had somehow been necessary – in order to maintain my image of myself as young and powerful – to keep Quintana a baby, dependent on me."

"That's a very powerful insight," he said. "There's something more in it. You're not the only one with an investment in her being dependent. She has her own investment."

I said that we had always – or at least for some years now – recognized her dependency, but we had always thought of it as primarily "her" problem, "our" problem only in the sense that it affected her and we had somehow failed to prevent it, failed to push her out of the nest.

" 'Push' is a telling word to use there. Most children don't need to be pushed from the nest. They can hardly wait to fly. They try it, they look back at their mothers, they see it's OK, they fly."

I said I didn't know at what point Quintana had become afraid to fly. As a young child and adolescent she was so physically fearless and independent that we would have laughed at any suggestion she might be dependent. The saucer at Lake Tahoe. Taking the Volvo at 14.

"She was definitely trying to fly. Do you think she looked back at you and saw it wasn't OK?"

I said this would suggest I had maintained a constant focus on her.

"Didn't you?"

I said no, not at all, a lot of the time I was working, even when I was physically present my work tended to isolate me.

"I think even when you were working you were focused on her. You were feeling guilty, you weren't giving her enough, there wasn't enough time. You told me yourself how sad it had made you when her friends were quoting their mothers' favorite sayings and she said yours was 'brush your teeth, brush your hair, shush I'm working.'"

That was true, I said. It was also true that all of my fiction during her childhood could be read as an attempt to work through separation from her before it happened. I had worked all that through. So why couldn't I separate?

Separation has everything to do with engagement, he said. You have trouble engaging. Maybe you dealt with her at a distance.

I said I dealt with everybody at a distance.

"Absolutely you do," he said. "It's the way you were brought up." He started talking again about John McCain's book. "I've only been able to read it in very short sections," he said. "It's too . . ."

Too what, I said.

He pointed at himself. "Too close."

I said I had read part of it, and saw what he meant. I had recognized myself in what he said about his family, his early life.

"Certain kinds of American families discourage open expression," he said. "He grew up in one of them, I did too, you did too. You have trouble talking to people one on one. You weren't brought up to do that."

I started to cry.

"Some people who were brought up this way are sufficiently sensitive that they can't talk to other people without crying," he said.

"As you can see," I said.

After a pause I asked if he thought I should talk to Quintana about any of this.

"I certainly think you should talk to her about how much trouble you have," he said.

"I don't want her to think she's causing me trouble," I said.

"No. Of course not. I mean how much trouble you have just talking to people. That has nothing to do with her, but it may open ways for her to understand certain things about you and her. She's probably very afraid of your being lonely. She has reason to be. You're obviously very close to your husband, but what would happen to you if something happened to him?"

I said she did seem to be afraid of that. She had expressed it. It had surprised me. I would have thought she'd be more worried about what would happen to you if something happened to me.

"Well, talk to her about it. You've got to start talking about these things. I can imagine how difficult it was for you to come in here and start talking to me. Just as difficult as it was for you to talk to that woman at Berkeley in 1955. A whole hour, one on one, no fixed agenda. You're forced to let your own agenda emerge.

You weren't ready to let your agenda emerge in 1955. I think you are now."

1-20-55

Started talking about never being good enough to satisfy. Doctor suggested that perhaps one learns early that others cannot be pleased. Thought of father but skipped over this. Talked about never belonging to a group, even though superficially accepted, never ignored by relatives – some confusion between doctor and me as to what "ignore" signifies. As an example I told her about feeling myself an outsider at my own sixth grade birthday party, even though it was a surprise party planned by my friends. I couldn't explain why. Doctor kept pressing point as if I must know and wouldn't tell her. Finally told her the others had stayed for dinner and I had not. This was partially untrue in a factual sense – it was something I thought at the time, but I see no reason in retrospect why they would give me a party just to exclude me from dinner. Doctor began talking about why I felt alienated from peer group. I said I thought it was because of moving around, also because of money – told her I always thought we were on brink of poverty – related example – how defensive my father's attitude is about money – of 500 Hawthorn Road and the "no swimming pool" to Jimmy and the "help with the gardening" to me. Unable to control effect of this on me, although the effect – extreme upset – has no rational basis.

Doctor brought up idea that I still seemed to very much need approval from my father – that perhaps I was as sparing with self-approval as he was of approval for me.

I said that this should not be so.

She implied that nonetheless it was, and said that I had "handed over a great deal of power to him."

Power over my own life? Something I had not considered before, set me slightly off-balance.

Discussed self-approval. Doctor defined it as the ability to feel comfortable with oneself. I said for me it would be the ability to make a decision with confidence that at least one of the choices was right. I said for example there seemed to be no right choices on this question of moving out of the Tri Delt house. If I didn't, I was stuck in an impossible situation. If I did, I was upsetting my father, they would take back my pin, etc. Maybe the thing to do was just withdraw, go home to Sacramento State.

"The central issue would seem to be, what do you *want* to do?"

I had to say I didn't know. Every road was fraught with doubt.

She brought up the "take back the pin" question.

I explained the procedure. I said that although I thought it was ridiculous and certainly couldn't care on a rational level whether or not I had a Tri Delt pin, there was something about it – like being excluded from a group to which I didn't want to belong – that made me fear it might have some effect later on.

"I should think that it would."

This startled me. I said nothing.

"It reminds me of a birthday party, you know? Everyone else sitting down to dinner together?"

I began to cry and then it was time to go.

3-29-55

First: "I don't know what to say."

"Why don't you say what you're thinking?"

"I'm only thinking I don't know what to say."

"Maybe that in itself needs to be said."

"One thing I've thought about – at the end of the last hour you said that admitting one was sorry would be a luxury. At the time I thought I understood, but now I don't – I mean I know that it would be a luxury, but I don't see why. A few nights ago I was lying in bed and I couldn't stop imagining that my father had died. I got very upset. I couldn't rationally overcome this feeling of intense guilt at not having made everything up to him before it was too late. The obvious answer to this would be for me – when

I did see him – to break down the barriers and say I'm sorry. But this answer seems just another refusal of responsibility on my part."

"Why that?"

"Because it's such a thing. Such a wild emotional giving up. And so impossible. It couldn't be done."

"Why not?"

"You just wouldn't do it in my family, or in anyone's. But I want so to do it before it's too late."

"This seems to be a feeling you have about a lot of things. I'm reminded of your remark at the beginning of the hour, when you didn't know what to say – wanting to make use of the time and being very conscious of the time slipping by. You seem to feel that way in so many situations – the feeling that it's going to be too late for you to do anything, that you're not going to come through, in a way."

"Yes. That's just it. And here, it's that the time is passing, I'm wasting your time. It's the same at home – I'm always conscious of the time passing and my being no further along toward righting the situation. And still, anytime my father asks me a question, I can only answer in monosyllables. . . . I want to tell the whole world I'm sorry and I don't know for what. And it can't be done, of course."

"I want you to understand that it's no personal disappointment to me or to any of us here if you fail to put your thoughts in words. It might well be, however, to yourself?"

"I know that. But I suppose I do feel that you expect something of me, even though I *know* that the loss is only my own."

" 'Only'?"

"Well, not anyone else's."

"Let's say, even if it were – for some reason – a personal disappointment to me, what difference would it make to you? You never agreed to become articulate with me. I never asked it, even supposing that I might expect it."

"That's it. It's the expectations that are unstated – they can never ever be met, because they can never really be known. There's always the possibility of some greater expectation."

"You seem to be leaving out the possibility that even if you did know what was expected – and even if you could meet those expectations – you might not want to."

"I can deal with the little expectations – the stated ones. I could meet them or refuse to meet them. But the others – the ones you don't know the reasons for – they have to be met. I can't refuse them. They become a necessity."

"I can understand that."

15 March 2000

Last week, I said, I said I had realized that I had a certain investment in Quintana's dependency. If Quintana was dependent on me, I was still young, still powerful, her mother. I thought when I said it that it had to do with my getting older, needing to feel that I was still in an earlier stage of my life. I have thought more about this, I said, and it seems to me now that I had always – even when I was much younger – had this investment in her dependency.

That seems very clear to me, he said.

That's what he meant, I said, when he said last week that of course I had always been working. He was saying that her dependency on me made me feel less guilty about working.

Go on, he said.

That didn't immediately work for me, I said. Because the fact is I never ever felt guilty about working.

I didn't say you felt guilty about working, he said. I said you felt guilty, and I said you worked. I left you to connect the two in whatever way you could.

There is a connection, I said. I felt guilty about not engaging, not being there emotionally. Working was what I did instead of engaging. Working, as you once pointed out, was the way I had found to not be there emotionally.

You had this very successful other place to go, he said. You created this place where you didn't have to engage. You created another world. And were rewarded for it. I would guess you were finding refuge in this alternate world from the time you were a very young child.

I had my office, I said. I can remember going into my office in the middle of parties at our house. Not to work. I would just go into my office and sit at my desk to be alone. I said we all, in our family, liked to be alone. Including Quintana. Even as a very small child she would become fretful if too many people were around her for too long. Put her in her room for a nap, however, and she would immediately seem happy as a bird, not napping, just talking and playing by herself. And later. Still. She can't be a house guest or have a friend stay with her for more than a night at the longest. She seems to need to be alone.

You all had your own rooms to go to, he said.

I said that this whole question of space, of rooms, had become very upsetting to me this week. I found myself very apprehensive about taking this trip to California with Quintana. She had said to begin with that she hoped we would each have our own room. I had said of course we would. I had gotten a suite with an adjoining bedroom. Then I started worrying – did the adjoining room actually connect? And when our assistant checked, it didn't. And I went crazy. Reacted out of all proportion until finally I got it worked out so that we would have two rooms that were separate but connected.

This is right on point, he said. The question of separate but connecting. That's where the two of you are trying to get, isn't it? To a point where you're separate but connected? Each free of the other, but each with a connection to each other?

I see that point, I said, but there was something else. I told him the "rehearsal dinner" playlet. I said I didn't think it would have upset me if I had been going alone – it just fed directly into my apprehension about the trip.

"It wouldn't have upset you that your mother didn't think your brother should see you as part of the family?"

Oddly enough, I said, I don't think it would have. This was all in my mind about wanting everything to be all right for Quintana. And, on reflection, I still don't know why I'm so worried about it. She seems to be doing very well. She's calm, she's open, she seems to have weathered the bad patches she went through, she joined a gym and is working out religiously after work – I think to fill that time when the old natural thing to do would be to have a drink – she's going regularly to a small group the head of Smithers put together. All this sounds good to us.

It sounds very good, he said. I think once she catches up with her chronological age, she's going to be fine.

I don't know exactly what you mean but it interests me, I said. It interests me because I've always thought she was a little slow catching up with her age. She didn't figure out how to be in high school until she was a senior. She was really on top of her game that year, and then she went to college and into free fall. Her last year at Barnard she was finally on top of that, but then she was out, and another free fall. I don't think she's learned yet how to be an adult. Do you think all along I was holding her back, keeping her dependent?

No, he said. The fact that you did or did not have an investment in her dependency doesn't mean she wasn't dependent to begin with. Nurture is a lot, but it isn't everything. There are certainly areas in which we're programmed genetically to act a certain way, to cope, not cope, whatever we do. I'm not saying that because she's adopted. Every time a sperm meets an egg you get a different set of genetic possibilities.

JDD: I don't see how you can say that and still say that John McCain has a lot of anger – by which you mean he feels guilty because he can never live up to the expectations on which he was raised. You're saying John McCain reacts the way he does because of nurture, you can't turn around and say Quintana reacts the way she does because of her genetic programming.

RMK: Of course nurture comes into play. I'm just saying so does the throw of the dice. We don't know about John McCain's siblings, for example. They haven't come to our attention. Which would suggest they may not be driven by whatever drives him. Same parents, different programming. You see it all the time in families.

At which point we began talking about families, my brother and I, my brother and his relationship with his children, Quintana's relationship with his children. I said I thought those children had been encouraged growing up to see one another as potential threats, and this extended to Quintana, so they had never been close. I said she had always been closer to your nieces and nephews, particularly to Dominique. I talked again about her insistence on going to school all the week Dominique was on life support, her refusal to be part of what amounted to a death watch.*

She couldn't deal with it, he said.

Obviously, I said. And we had to deal with it, we couldn't focus on trying to help her through it. We did, the day after the funeral, go to Hawaii with her, and we were able to talk about it some there. One thing I've never talked to her about is whether it affected her attitude toward boys, men, boyfriends. Did it make her at some level distrustful. Would that seem possible to you?

I don't think at sixteen, he said. By the time you're sixteen you've figured out how you feel about the opposite sex. Much earlier experiences go into determining those attitudes.

Then, I said, there was a whole unpleasantness afterwards. I explained about the trial, the possible plea bargain, Nick's attitude and fury at us.

"You thought things would come out in a trial that wouldn't be good," he said. "And he thought it would all go his way."

Yes, I said. I explained about Quintana and me being on the witness list, and sending Quintana away, going away ourselves.

* Dominique Dunne was taken off life support five days after she was strangled by her former boyfriend, who was tried and convicted of voluntary manslaughter. Dominique's family believed that the judgment should have been more severe. Her father, Nick Dunne, wrote about the trial for *Vanity Fair*.

"And he wanted you to stay there and testify, under the misunderstanding that it would help convict her killer."

I said he even wanted his fragile middle son to testify, despite the fact that the incident he was to testify about had been witnessed by him during a weekend when he was on leave from Silver Hill, where he was being treated for paranoid schizophrenia.

"I can see your frustration," he said.

22 March 2000

I said that what had been most on my mind this week was the discussion we had had with Quintana first on Thursday at dinner and then Sunday over lunch. I explained: she said that she was talking about this earlier than she had meant to because she had or was expecting to have an offer to change jobs, go to a new magazine in more or less the same position but at a much higher salary. This had precipitated her asking herself if she really wanted to keep on doing the same thing, if this might not be the time to strike out on her own, try just taking pictures.

In the first place, he said, on the face of it there are two separate issues here. She might decide not to take the new job and still not think the time is right to strike out on her own. That's an unrelated decision, one she could act on or defer.

I said I thought we had tried to make some such point. I said that although we both supported the idea that she should be taking pictures on her own, we had some reservations about her doing it now. She had tried to do this at an earlier point, when she was a few years out of school and had been working for a photo agency, and after a year she had taken a magazine job. I said I had mentioned to her at dinner that in retrospect this had been the period when drinking became a problem to her, and she had said no, the problem hadn't been drinking, the problem had been D. I explained about the relationship with D. I said that drinking had in fact been a big part of it, that his wanting her to stay over into the week in Riverdale – which she saw as counterproductive to her work – had in fact involved a lot of drinking, which, by her own account at the time, was all he did on weekends.

"He wanted a drinking buddy," he said.

Something like that, I said. This was confirmed last summer, when she was in detox at Millstein and ran into him. "I guess we both always knew it would come to this," she reported his saying.

"How exactly did you think it would be helpful to her to mention this," he asked.

I said I could see after the fact that it hadn't been helpful. That she had taken it in good spirit, but I shouldn't have said it. I had just thought at the time it was something she should be aware of, on guard against, so it didn't sideswipe her.

"What do you think the subtext of the entire conversation was," he asked.

I said that for me, it was about dependency. Obviously, although it went undiscussed, going out on her own would involve financial dependency on us. I was very afraid that this would exacerbate her feelings of dependency, which were at the very heart of where she was now.

"That's at the bottom of it all right," he said. "It's a very tricky thing to negotiate. It's very hard to conceive of financial support as not involving strings. Some very lucky people who are born to some extraordinary parents seem to be able to transcend the strings. But most of us see them. You're going to have to talk about that, but delicately. You're going to have to find a way to say that the money would be hers anyway. I'm assuming this won't mean financial hardship for you."

I said not really. At any rate it wasn't in the short term our primary concern.

"Maybe the way to do it is to say, look, this would have been yours someday, we're giving it to you now because now is when you need it."

"Phrase it as an investment," I suggested.

"Well, yes, but not exactly. With an investment, you expect a return. You have to be clear that any return you expect is intangible. You want her to have this when you're alive to enjoy seeing her use it to grow."

I said that I had been further troubled by what I interpreted as a kind of regression or resistance in these two discussions. Her focus seemed to be on leaving her job rather than on going somewhere specific. We had talked about taking it step by step, things she had to do, she had to get a book together, how long that would take, she had to draw up lists of people to see, agents, editors, etc. The more we talked, the less she seemed to offer.

"Because you were infantilizing her," he said. "She isn't some little girl just out of school, you have to tell her she should get a book together. She knows she has to have a book. She's been on the other side of the desk. She knows far more about this than you do."

"Then why hasn't she done it already," I asked.

"I don't know. Has she ever exhibited her photographs?"

I said not really, she never got them together. A friend of ours [Earl]* who had a gallery had seen some of her pictures and told her she should get more together and he would show them, but she never had. Similarly, several friends of ours who were well-known professional photographers had repeatedly said she should call them, but she never did.

"Why do you think she didn't," he said.

I said I think she's afraid to show her work. She's afraid of rejection, afraid someone won't like it. I said I could understand this very well. I told him about getting the letter from Robert Lescher[†] when I was at Berkeley and never answering it. I

* Earl McGrath was one of Didion's closest friends until his death in 2016. He was a charismatic figure who moved easily between the worlds of music and art. They had become friends in the early 1960s when they lived in Los Angeles and remained friends when they moved to New York.
† Robert Lescher was an important editor and, later, literary agent in New York.

couldn't possibly have answered it, because he wanted to see my work, and I was afraid if I showed it he'd say it was bad and my whole little secret dream of being a writer would be over.

"I think you have to tell Quintana that story," he said. "I think it would be very meaningful to her. The conversation you have to have with her isn't about why she didn't do this, why she never finished that. Your message can't be 'why don't you ever finish anything.' The conversation has to address these underlying fears she has. If she knew that you felt the same way, and yet you overcame it, it could be very good for her. There's a lot here she has to understand. She has to understand that artistic achievement involves showing the work, putting yourself on the line. She has to understand that the world doesn't end if some people don't like it."

I said I would think she already understood that, since she'd been watching us put ourselves on the line and reading our bad reviews her entire life.

"You don't understand," he said. "You think she sees you as you see yourself, somebody who overcame a lot of fears to get where you are. I suspect that you and your husband also see yourselves as extremely lucky, in that each has the other to support your risks, make them in effect less risky. She doesn't see you that way. She sees you as some exalted supertalented being. She thinks you were born the way you are now, programmed from conception to succeed. I think you need to talk to her about the support you and your husband give each other, about the support you get from editors or whoever, about how your first bad review made you feel, your first turndown – about everything that went into getting where you are, about being afraid you wouldn't make it. Tell her that story about the agent."

I said I thought it would be enormously helpful to her to find a professional mentor. Someone she would want to please, someone who would expect things from her.

"Absolutely it would," he said. "Someone outside the family. And at the moment, Dr. Kass is playing that role. Perfect transference. Then she can resent him. Seriously, I think this whole area presents a tremendous opportunity for growth on her part. The trick for you, obviously, is in how you guide her through it."

19 April 2000

I said that the benefits to me of the 5 days with Quintana had seemed to continue – I felt easier about her, less concerned about not seeing or hearing from her, more comfortable about letting her work this out alone.

"She's not trying to exclude the two of you," he said. "I hope you're beginning to see that. She needs the relationship very much, she craves it. But she needs time alone, she needs space, she needs to look in the mirror and not see herself through your and your husband's eyes. I don't mean this just as a metaphor. It's literal too. You must have had the experience of seeing yourself on television or hearing yourself on tape and thinking that can't be me, I don't look that way, I don't sound that way. Then you get used to yourself and it's all right. She doesn't know yet how she sounds or looks. She's working on learning that."

I said we had become aware that she tended to read our questions to her as nagging, or trying to control, which triggered a defensive reaction from her.

"She very definitely reads you – both of you – that way. She thinks you ask questions because you don't trust her. She thinks you don't trust her to do what she has to do. And her automatic defense is not to do what you suggest. She'll cut off her nose to spite her face if you tell her not to. I'm not saying this out of some special knowledge of her, I'm saying it because it's the characteristic dynamic between parents and grown children who have not yet effected a healthy separation. I must have told you this in one way or another fifty times, but you had to see it for yourself."

I said that over the course of the five days we spent together I had at first made a conscious effort not to ask her anything that might trigger the defensiveness. And that she had become more open, even volunteered information I had avoided asking her about.

"She got the idea. She recognized you didn't undertake this trip as a way of trying to slip past her very fragile defenses, and she responded with gratitude. I hope your husband is beginning to understand this too, because you both need to loosen your attachment to her. Not the attachment that says you love her, but the attachment that says you need to run her life because she can't run it herself."

I said that you did understand it, although you had not had the benefit of the five days alone, which in terms of how I felt had been quite liberating. I felt as if a great deal of worry and confusion had begun to lift.

"If your husband still feels that worry and confusion, bring him in with you. I think the important thing for both of you to remember is that laying any stress on Quintana right now will be counterproductive. She needs to learn who she is before she can learn to handle stress."

I said we were trying to avoid things that had caused stress in the past. For example, the idea of going to St. Barth's for Thanksgiving had last year been – according to Dr. Kass – a source of some stress. I had talked to her about it, trying to de-stress it by saying it made no difference to us, we knew it might be a hard time at work, all we needed was word one way or another 4 weeks before the fact so that we could cancel her room. I had then reminded her of this at the 4 week point, and she said she had thought it through and decided she wanted to go. Then we didn't go because of the hurricane, and in some ways it had been a relief – some measure of ambiguity was still present, and we didn't want to see it kick in once we got there or after.

So. This year we had decided to go instead to Paris, where we could cancel her room at the last minute, she could be more independent, etc.

"Why take her at all?"

Because it's a holiday, I said. I don't want her to feel left out.

"Why would she feel left out? Doesn't she have her own life? Isn't it time she started living it? It's not like the two of you are running off on vacation and leaving a five-year-old alone at Christmas, is it?"

I said I just didn't want her to be lonely.

"What makes you assume she'd be lonely? Would you have been lonely at her age if your mother and father had taken a trip at Thanksgiving without you?"

Of course not, I said. At her age I was married and had her. We had our own holidays. We went very occasionally to your family or mine but this was more a duty than what we really preferred doing.

"I know you grew up in a big extended family. I suspect your husband did too. I did, most of us did. But life has changed."

I said life had changed for those of us who left. The big extended families more or less went on as before. For example – at Lori's wedding – all my cousins were saying that we had to come to Easter this year because the next generation was doing it, we should all turn out. This was by no means a case of their all still living in Sacramento – they had scattered as far away as New Jersey, but they were all going to Easter at Niffer's. They had a lot of events like this. They had the lunch at the Clift the Saturday before Christmas, they had Easter, etc. I said Quintana had been mystified by this, because we lived so differently. Her father and I had both left.

"You left physically, yes, but you just said, that wasn't the issue. One of your cousins lives in New Jersey, but she goes to Easter. She goes to the Christmas lunch at the Clift. You don't."

I said I had also left emotionally. So had you.

"Why did you leave," he asked. "Did you feel that your families in some way impinged on your freedom? Did you feel that if you didn't make the break they would try to control you?"

60

I said I didn't know. I supposed to some extent yes.

"What's interesting here is that you both broke, but then you seem to have created the same kind of family."

"On a very small scale, I suppose so."

"You don't think the small scale magnifies the power to control?"

I said I got the point.

"Just give her room. Respect her. Let her see herself as she is. The more she looks at herself through her own eyes, the better she'll like what she sees. You had to learn to see yourself with your own eyes. I would be very surprised to learn that public appearances were not in the beginning very difficult for you. But you got used to it. You learned to like yourself."

I said on the whole yes, I had gotten used to it. Except every once in a while, out of nowhere, I would get stage fright to the point of paralysis, throwing up. The rest of the time I could just go on, do it, even enjoy it.

"Think about those times when you couldn't. Did they have anything in common?"

I thought about this while walking to get the bread. There was the public lecture at Berkeley in 1975. There was the PEN reading here in the theater. There was also a lecture I gave once at Davis. While I was waiting for the bread to be wrapped I got it. The Davis lecture, which was a nothing occasion, no freight, was the key. On each of these occasions – and on no others – one or both of my parents had been present.

26 April 2000

Dr. MacKinnon asked how Easter was. I said it was really good, and Monday and early Tuesday I had actually begun to feel slightly in charge, almost euphoric.

Then what happened, he asked.

I explained what happened. From the initial call to Sharon[*] through the call from St. Monica's through your meeting her and our talking through last evening and this morning. That she hadn't eaten in three days and hadn't slept the night before. That she said she couldn't stand lying to everyone anymore. That she had cut off contact with the people who cared about her – because she was afraid they would intervene, "put her in a looney bin" – and had been exclusively seeing people who didn't care about her.

Which made her hate herself, see herself as worthless, he said.

Yes, I said. To the point where she said several times that she would be better off not existing. Which seemed to us extremely dangerous.

"It is extremely dangerous," he said. "There's a high correlation of chronic alcoholism to suicide. I can't tell you strongly enough, you have to play every card you have with her – play the guilt card, play it shamelessly – tell her you would never have another good day if anything happened to her. If ever there was a time to make her feel she has to take care of you, protect you, this is it. I've treated suicidal patients, I've been on the inside of this, I know how they think, they manage to convince themselves that everyone they love would be better off without them, would get over it, would be better off not having to worry any more. You have to disabuse her of this in the strongest possible way."

* Didion and Dunne's assistant.

I said we had tried to do this. I said that at one point when she had said she would be better off not existing I had told her if she didn't exist I couldn't live. Then you had come into the kitchen where she and I were hugging each other and crying and I had told you what we were talking about. And you had said, lightening the moment, "and of course I'd be just fine," and she had laughed and said "oh right, you'd just sail through it."

"This sounds encouraging, a very healthy conversation," he said.

I said that she and I had talked about Dr. Kass. Both in California and last night she had said that Dr. Kass seemed to be distancing himself from her. I learned last night that she had in fact told Dr. Kass that this wasn't working, that she wanted to see him only every two weeks. I asked her if Dr. Kass knew she was drinking. She said no, "he never asks me." I had suggested that this might be the cause of what she construed as distance. That there was between them in every conversation this secret she wouldn't trust him with, and he might well be sensing the obstacle. "Now that you say it," she had said to me, "of course that's it, it's perfectly clear." Then I think you should tell him, I had said. It's all part of not lying any more. She had agreed.

"I suggested to you once that it might be useful for me to mention this to Dr. Kass, and you didn't want me to," he said "Have you changed your mind at all?"

I said I didn't think so. I might well feel differently if she hadn't talked to him about it by next week. But I thought the value here was in her telling him – her being honest – rather than in my intervening, robbing her of the chance to be honest.

"I see some wisdom in that," he said. "We can see what happens when they next meet."

I told him about the Hazelden Parents' Week discussion. I said that of course we had been busy, but that quite frankly there had also been an element of simply not wanting to go. Not being trapped in a five-day situation (she said 3, my recollection is 5, which tallies more with Parents' "Week") with people we didn't know and didn't much want to share our concerns with. I could do the reading alone. I could get it without being lectured to. It would be one long Al-Anon meeting, no out.

"The value of those programs isn't in what you learn or don't learn about alcoholism, although that's what they tell you," he said. "The value is in the statement. You're telling the child by your presence not just that you take the problem seriously – you already made that statement, by taking her there – but that you take this specific solution seriously. You're in effect legitimizing it. That can be very meaningful to someone who has looked to you for cues her entire life."

I said maybe we had made a mistake, but it was hard for me to see it as such after hearing last night about the pressure they put on Quintana to get us there – "don't you feel angry your parents won't come?" and asking her if you were an alcoholic when she said she couldn't really see you having a 6 pm dinner without two scotches.

This really made him laugh. "It might have been helpful if you went," he said, "but of course her bringing it up last night was partly based on looking to assign blame to someone else."

I said this had been your reaction, as re Nicola, and told her about Nicola.

"Getting honest with yourself is hard in general, and it's harder still for alcoholics, because lying has become so deeply integrated into their personality structure. There's a lot of work to be done. But on the whole I could interpret this as a very positive development – she's trying to confront it, she came to the right people, you supported her, everybody's talking. It's when she pulls back – stops talking – that you're in trouble again."

I said that she had given me "The Big Book" last night, and that I had read it, and there had been some quite interesting things in it. I said I had come to see the point in some of the steps, for example the fourth step, which involved listing your resentments and analyzing each resentment for the threat it masked.

"Did she see you reading it? Did she know you read it?"

I said yes. I had read her some parts of it at breakfast this morning, and we had discussed them. She was concerned because she had not completed the "homework" for her Big Book meeting, which involved doing this fourth step, after which, according to Bill W., "you will have swallowed big hunks of truth about yourself." I had told her that in the state she had been in, she had been in no way ready to swallow big hunks of truth about herself. I had told her that now she might be ready, and that this was something to talk to the man from Smithers about. We had also discussed the order of the steps. It seemed to me they were in the wrong order – that you could get to the "higher power" step (2 or 3) by understanding of the later steps, but it was a hopeless leap of faith where it was. I didn't understand why you had to do them in order, but she said you did.

"You don't. You take them any way they work for you. But that was very useful to her. To see you reading and absorbing and taking it seriously. The more discussions like that you have, the more hope there is that she can follow through. There's something you should consider, however. She may need to be detoxed. She may not be able to tolerate withdrawal on her own. This is something you need to watch, and discuss. Because when the blood alcohol drops, she may need a drink. And then, without help, she's back where she was. You have to keep on top of this, because if she's not drinking, it could happen quite soon."

I said we would be aware of that, and that there was something else specific I wanted his advice on. As we had discussed, she had expressed a strong wish several weeks ago to leave her job, go out on her own as a photographer. We had responded to this positively. No action had been taken, however, and it didn't, for obvious reasons, come up last night. What I wanted to ask was this: given the situation as revealed last night, would we be wrong – if the question came up anytime within the next several weeks – to discourage the move?

"No. You wouldn't be wrong. It's absolutely the wrong time for her to be waking up alone every morning having to reinvent her life. She probably realizes that – which is why no action has been taken – but if she doesn't, you have to find a way to tell her. I assume you've already talked to her about the things we talked about – the need, if she's going to live that kind of life, to accept the risk of criticism? To accept the fact that she has to put her ego on the line?"

I said we had talked about it at some length in California. At only one point she had become defensive, saying "does that mean you won't support me?", but I had talked her through that, and we had had what I thought were good talks about it.

"I think what you have to do when and if this comes up in the immediate future is set a condition on her doing it. Explain your concerns, of course. But don't pin it to some ideal of sobriety which right now is beyond the horizon to her. Say that she'll be ready to handle the demand of the life when she completes some professional task that, given her fears of criticism – which she construes as failure – will entail putting herself on the line to some extent. If she got together a show of her work, for example, then she would be ready – because she would have already accepted the risk of criticism."

3 May 2000

I said I was very depressed. I said there didn't seem to be anything you or I could do to help Quintana. When I last saw him we were in a crisis situation, but we were – or had been as of noon that day – talking openly.

"Then she withdrew," he said.

Yes, I said. And I had looked back over this chronology I had made of events since last summer and saw that this had been a pattern. Every 4-6 weeks a crisis, an opening, then the withdrawal, the distancing.

"But that's natural," he said. "That's absolutely to be expected. You don't see that?"

I said I had begun to feel she was setting us up to respond a certain way.

"She is. That's been the nature of your relationship. That's what we're trying to break. We're trying to teach you not to respond as expected. She comes to you for help, you give it, she rejects it, you show your disappointment. Is that how it played out in this instance?"

I said more or less, yes. I explained about the call to Robert.* I said that we had discussed the possibility of her talking to him during this crisis, and she had seemed open to this idea. But we had not called him until after we had discussed it again with her on Sunday night.

"Why not," he asked.

I said there had been another recent instance in which we had suggested she talk to someone, she had agreed, the call had been

* Robert Fox is an English film and theater producer. He was briefly married to Natasha Richardson. Their wedding took place in the Didion/Dunne apartment in New York.

made, and then she had never followed up. It had become kind of an issue, in our minds if not necessarily in hers.

"Believe me, if it was an issue in your minds, it was an issue in her mind. Her refusal to follow through in the previous instance suggests pretty clearly that she felt pushed, crowded."

"But she had agreed that this previous call be made."

"Because it was easier? Because she didn't want an argument?"

In retrospect, I said, that had obviously been the case. Which was why, in this second instance, we wanted to be absolutely sure that she wanted us to make the call. You had asked her (A) if she wanted to talk to Robert (the answer was "I would love to"), and (B) in that case, did she prefer that she make the initial call or would she like you to call first? The answer to this was that she wanted you to call first. So, on Monday morning, you had made the call, then left the information on her answering machine. But by Tuesday morning she had not made the call, and when asked about it last night said that she had made the call but they had missed each other. Then had become resistant, conveying pretty clearly that she felt pushed. Which I didn't think was fair to us, or truthful with herself.

"Fairness doesn't come into this," he said. "Alcoholics aren't truthful with themselves, that's what defines the illness. You have to work around them, outwit them, somehow enlist them in their own recovery."

I said that's what we had been trying to do. That's specifically why we had asked her to confirm her interest in this. I asked him how he would have handled it.

"In this first place, I would have suggested that only one of you – you or your husband – be involved in this negotiation with her. That would make it harder for her to jump to what has by now become reflexively her readiest conclusion, that there's a united front – the two of you together, her friends, Dr. Kass, whoever is at the moment exhibiting concern – trying to manage her life. In the second place, I would probably have suggested that the negotiator on this be you. Daughters in our culture tend to perceive their mothers as less potentially controlling than their fathers. Sons, on the other hand, tend to perceive their fathers as less potentially controlling than their mothers. These perceptions may or may not be mistaken, but I've found them fairly persistent in the family dynamic. Third, I would have suggested that the negotiation go a lot further than it did. You went as far as asking if she wanted to make the initial call or have you do it. When she said she wanted you to do it, I would have then asked if she wanted to be in the room when you made the call. If she said no, I would have then asked for her advice on what to say, how to tell it. And if she said it didn't matter to her what you said, I would have laughed, passed it off, made a joke of it, said something like 'would I be reading you correctly if I thought you don't care what I say because you're not going to follow up anyway?' "

I said this was all very hard on both you and me. It made it almost impossible to do any sustained work – even not sustained work – in the middle of a work discussion one or the other of us would revert to talking about Quintana.

"That's very bad. Because work is an extremely effective anti-anxiety agent. As you know. You've certainly used it as such all your life, and it's worked for you. A lot of your anxiety now has to do with not working."

I said yes, of course. And there were a lot of other irritations and problems going on in our work life. A very badly handled contract for example.

"Don't you have agents who can take that over for you, considering what else you have to worry about?"

I said agents didn't really do it. Our lawyer had for decades done it, but he was now in his late eighties, his wife was ill, he wasn't entirely on the situation and the other people in his office weren't up to it.

"So you have some decisions to make, and you don't feel up to making them."

Exactly, I said. And we would have to be the ones to make them, because any thought that our lawyer would make the decision for us had more or less been banished when his firm broke up at Christmas and he formed a new one.

"You have a lot to handle here. I think I'd like you to try another anti-depressant. I think we have to get you working effectively again."

He then asked if I was still worried about suicide. I said yes, to the point where I was slightly concerned about going to Washington this weekend for even one night.

"Then don't go," he said.

I said I had to go, and in any case, if I didn't go, I probably wouldn't talk to Quintana all weekend anyway and then I'd end up mad at her for disrupting my life.

"You make the mistake of thinking this is about Quintana. It's not. It's about you. Nothing anyone does or doesn't do can keep someone from hurting herself if she gets it fixed in her mind to do so. All you can do is save yourself from undue guilt. Satisfy yourself that you did all you could. If you truly think you could save her by not going to Washington, don't go. If you can truly accept that it wouldn't make any difference, then go."

I said I could truly accept that it wouldn't make any difference, and in any case, if anything happened there would be too much else to feel guilty about.

"That's true. People even feel guilt about accidents over which they had no control. Why did I let her take that trip. Why did she

70

take that particular car. Why did we have a swimming pool, why did we go to the lake."

I said I had been unable to banish – this week – the persistent thought I had mentioned to him before, that all of her guilt and lying about drinking may be unnecessary, may be the result of having "defined" her drinking as a problem.

"I think her drinking is a definite problem. I've never seen a true alcoholic who could drink in moderation."

Maybe it was situational, I suggested. Maybe her situation would change and she'd cut back on drinking, if nobody had ever called her an alcoholic. Who defines a "true alcoholic"?

"Well, the AMA definition would probably include 50% of this country, and 100% of France. But in general we define alcoholic drinking as drinking exclusively to sedate, to allay anxiety, to counter depression, to sleep. There are two most common forms. One is the person who starts drinking in the morning to allay anxiety – he's never drunk, but he's never far from a drink. The other is the binge drinker."

I said I wondered if her drinking wasn't more the way mine was when I was in my twenties, before I was married and had a child. I drank at lunch, I went to cocktail parties and I drank, I continued drinking through and after dinner – if dinner even entered the picture. Then my life changed and I just found myself drinking less.

"That was at a time and in a culture when everybody drank that way. You weren't drinking more than most people were. I remember as a young naval officer, if you were going to be late to the party you'd have two or three drinks on the way so you'd be caught up. This isn't that time. That's not the way she's drinking."

10 May 2000

I said that I had been unable to swallow Welbutrin, was taking Zoloft instead, and had noticed some increase in concentration and well-being.

"Do you ever wonder about this difficulty in swallowing," he asked.

Not really, I said. My father couldn't swallow pills. I had read that something like a third of all people couldn't swallow pills.

"That's true," he said, "but it's not inevitable, it's not like the common cold, there's a reason for it. Were you given pills as a little child?"

I said I didn't remember. *Actually, on thinking about it, I do remember. I was given aspirin to bring down a fever and my father told me not to try to swallow it, just chew it, it was easier.*

"Did it become something of an issue," he asked.

No, I said. Not like eating. Eating was an issue between me and my mother. I couldn't get up from the table until I'd cleaned my plate. This led to some long stretches of sitting at the table. *On thinking about it, my eating also became an issue between my mother and father. "If she doesn't feel like eating, don't make her eat," my father would say. "She's not a garbage can." These arguments could become quite pitched.*

"Some mothers are so controlling on this issue that they'll actually serve the child whatever was left uneaten at the next meal."

I said that my mother would in fact do that, but I hadn't thought of her as "controlling".

"Why not?"

I said that she was the opposite of the conventional personality that comes to mind with "controlling". She wasn't in any way compulsive about her house or her appearance. She never even made beds. Sometimes as a child I would clean the house because I just couldn't stand the mess anymore. She would always say don't bother with that, life is too short, let's do something we want to do, let's have a picnic. I remember being mortified by a picture taken on one such picnic because she hadn't bothered to braid my hair that morning – it was just the way I'd slept in it. Later in childhood, when I started sewing, she thought I was too much of a perfectionist, too compulsive about doing it right. A lot of areas like that, she'd say I was wasting time. She had always tended to think – and still did – that I put too much effort into things that didn't matter.

"You didn't see that as controlling? You didn't interpret her reaction as disapproval of your efforts, as an insistence that you do it her way?"

I said possibly, but it was an arcane way of "controlling". I said that as I became an adolescent, I had in fact thought her distrustful and overcritical – of my friends, of the way I dressed, etc. In fact she was still that way, but I didn't notice it anymore. Quintana had noticed it when we were in California, and had mentioned it to me. She said she thought I probably wouldn't have told my mother things. I said that I told her everything, until a certain point. "When you started to be independent," Quintana had said.

"Let's get back to this eating question. Was she concerned about your health?"

I said I supposed so. I was always underweight, at the beginning of World War Two I stopped growing for two years.

"Were you seen by a doctor? Was there a diagnosis?"

I said that my pediatrician had called it "failure to thrive", and said that I was sad, I missed my father, if my mother wanted me to eat we should join my father.

"You had an episode of childhood depression, in other words."

I said if children did have episodes of depression, I supposed so.

"Oh, they definitely do. It's quite common among children who perceive themselves as unable to please a critical or controlling parent."

I said I didn't understand where the impulse to protect ended and the impulse to control began. They seemed, for a parent, the same thing.

"That's probably the way it begins, yes. You have this totally helpless creature to protect. The ideal situation is when the mother senses the child's growing ability – and believe me, it grows by leaps and bounds—to make his or her own decisions. Parents who themselves grew up in controlling families tend to miss these cues, or to fear them. So they extend protection beyond the point where it's needed."

I said we realized that we had tended to overprotect Quintana.

"To the point where she interprets it as control," he said.

I said that this was very hard for me to sort out. Because clearly, she still needed protection.

"You can't protect her any more. It's not possible, it's beyond your capability. You can't do it, she doesn't need it. What she needs is your trust, your confidence that she's capable of making the right decisions for her. That's a different thing."

I told him about the dream I had this week in which Quintana and I were sharing a room and every time I woke during the night she wasn't in her bed, she was sitting by the window and she was getting drunker and drunker. And there was nothing I could do about it. She couldn't see me watching her.

"This is the hardest thing in the world, for a loving parent to relinquish the idea that he or she can protect his or her child. I think you need to spend more time alone with Quintana. You and your husband both, separately, although the mother-daughter relationship seems to be more troubling to her. That was a very acute thing she noticed about you and your own mother. She was way ahead of you there. These are things the two of you need to talk about."

17 May 2000

I said that I had stopped taking Zoloft on Friday May 12, because I had felt woozy after taking it Thursday and still felt that way Friday morning. After not taking it Friday the feeling cleared by midday, but that I missed it, because during the week I took it, it had actually improved my focus and well-being. Since stopping I again felt low, apprehensive, anxious.

He suggested that I resume it but halve the dose. Either a quarter tab every day or a half tab every other day. He said I had been taking a subclinical dose to begin with but clearly it had been too much.

I said I had read in this morning's paper about a new drug for alcoholism, not yet approved in the US but in trials. The trials were showing what were described as very good results with patients who really wanted to not drink.

He said he had heard about it on the radio this morning. The key point emphasized was that the good results were with people who wanted to stop drinking.

I said I didn't think that Quintana really wanted to stop. That she wanted not to have the bad results, but hadn't reached the point where she wanted not to drink.

"That's apparently true," he said. "There's no question, she is drinking. Dr. Kass knows it. The course he'll follow now is to work with her to isolate those times when it's impossible not to drink from the times when it's relatively easy, or at least possible, not to drink. And to get her to think about what characterizes those times. What makes them different."

I said we had dinner with her Sunday night, and she had mentioned talking about something like this to Dr. Kass. That he had apparently asked her when she wanted a drink and that she had said she wanted a drink every minute of every night. I said that you and I had different reactions to the evening. You had focused on her being more open than she had seemed the last few times we saw her. I, on the other hand – and this was what made me see that I was falling back into anxiety, had focused on the fact that I thought she was drinking. And that certain of her reactions had seemed to me what I had come to recognize as alcoholic. Her resentment of Kendall for doing the French West Indies for example, when she could well have done it herself had she taken the initiative – the last time you and I went to St. Barth's, the story was on the schedule, as yet unassigned, and I had suggested to her that she could fly down with us or apart from us, go to the other islands, join us or not as she liked – but that she hadn't asked Marian* about it.

"She still hasn't made any decision to change her work situation?"

She hasn't mentioned anything about it, I said. Nor have we mentioned it to her.

"Good," he said. "Obviously, if she reopens it, you talk about it. But she has to initiate it."

I said that I had been reading a book about the Rational Recovery movement. Many things about it seemed to resonate in terms of Quintana's situation and her reaction to AA, basically the rejection of the medical model for alcoholism. One of the things she had said many times in extremis was this: why do I have to be sick for the rest of my life? And each time I would say, you don't, you're not sick now, you certainly don't have to be sick for the rest of your life. And she would say, I am sick, I'm an alcoholic, I always will be, I'm sick. When I read AA literature, I saw that this was the message she was getting from AA. And it was giving her a good deal of trouble.

"I know, I know," Dr. MacKinnon said. "I once had a patient who had successfully stopped drinking, did AA, hadn't drunk in ten years, and still he kept referring to himself as a 'recovering

* Marian McEvoy was the editor of *Elle Decor*. She hired Quintana to work at the magazine and encouraged her work as a photographer.

alcoholic'. One day I said to him, I couldn't help myself, 'when, if not now, do you think you'll be 'recovered'? 'Never,' he said. 'Alcoholics never recover.' Through a great deal of work, I finally got him to see himself as recovered, not sick, over it, but I understand the difficulty she has with this."

I said that some time ago I had mentioned to Quintana that I had ordered this Rational Recovery book. She had heard about the movement and expressed interest in reading it when it came. But after I read it – despite the fact that it spoke very directly to much of her resistance – I never gave it to her or mentioned it again, because it was so hostile to AA – basically it suggested AA made you brain-dead – and I was still hoping she could find her way through AA. I did however think AA's medical model for alcoholism was a big mistake, in that it provided an excuse for drinking by insisting the "disease" was bigger than you were, beyond your control.

"The medical model isn't totally worthless. It began, of course, only as a way to destigmatize alcoholism. You're not a worthless drunk in the gutter, you have an illness like any other, it's not your fault. But, more recently, there's some evidence that there is a genetic component to alcoholism. Siblings who grow up adopted into demonstrably dissimilar circumstances tend to share genetically determined illnesses, and they also share alcoholism. But you can control most of these genetic predispositions. You can modify your behavior. Diabetes is genetic, but if you keep your weight down and watch your diet, you won't get it. If you have the enzyme that predisposes the carrier to lung cancer, you don't smoke. If you have a genetic tendency to alcoholism, you don't drink. What she needs to do is figure out the pattern of her need to drink, and try to eliminate or overcome those circumstances that provoke the need."

I said Mother had mentioned to me, before Lori's wedding, her concern that such a festive event would be very hard for Quintana. Which had seemed to me a total misunderstanding of why Quintana drank. She didn't drink to have a good time.

No, of course not, he said.

Yet I had mentioned this to Quintana, and she said that in fact the wedding had been very hard for her – that she had craved a drink – even plotted what to order – a rum and Coke that everybody would think was a Coke. All that had prevented her from satisfying this craving was that every time she was about to go to the bar, her cousin Stephen was there.

"Social events are really occasions of stress for most people. We find it so hard to communicate with one another that we need alcohol to get through it. Even now, when most of my contemporaries have medical conditions that prevent them from drinking, I see them at cocktail parties holding onto glasses of Perrier as if that can help them. Cocktail parties are really very demanding occasions."

I said that one of the beauties of life in California was that cocktail parties didn't exist. The distances were so great, and the way of life so Swiss, that you went to somebody's house for dinner at 7:30, left at 10:30, went to bed and got up early.

"How ideal," he said.

I said that Quintana – because she left California when she was still adolescent – had never gotten into this rhythm. She had complained Sunday night about a friend always calling on his way into town from the redeye, and the main objection seemed to be he woke her up, although she had then said he was bad for her, he did drugs, etc. It had concerned me a little – because it seemed an example of her cutting herself off from people who cared about her – and it had occurred to me to suggest that maybe he wasn't calling because he was selfish or because he didn't care about her, but precisely because he did care about her, that he wanted to keep in touch.

"What would you have hoped to accomplish by suggesting that?"

I said I didn't know, which was why I hadn't suggested it, but in general I supposed I would have hoped to make her realize that she wasn't necessarily the target, that other people she construed as plaguing her might have concerns of their own.

"Alcoholics very often exhibit paranoid thinking patterns. As you can imagine, I've had a lot of experience with clinical paranoia – and believe me, normal people who have gotten into even mild paranoid thinking patterns react the same way. They turn the paranoia on anyone who dares to suggest that they aren't the target. You're insulting their perception. You're saying their cognitive process is defective. The most I've ever been able to get away with saying is something along the lines of, 'Have any alternative interpretations occurred to you?' Paranoid thinking takes a lot of forms. Shyness is a form of paranoia. You assume you're the center of attention."

I said I had been extremely shy. But that in fact someone had once pointed out to me how silly it was to assume that everybody would be noticing me – and that it had helped me, been liberating. The occasion was in early adolescence. Jennie Clifton and I were all dressed up – stockings, high heels – to go to dinner with her mother in San Francisco. In the car I discovered a run in my stocking and was devastated. Jennie's mother had made fun of me, and it had been great.

"It can be, if you hit just the right tone, and it's just the right moment, but that's hard to do."

"Last week," I said, "we were discussing William Styron and you described him as very angry. You said that most depressives were very nice people – because they turned their anger on themselves – but that depressive alcoholics tended to turn their anger on other people. And I had said that I saw that in Quintana – there was a lot of misdirected anger at people at work, people on the street, etc. Then I had said 'I don't know what I mean by misdirected, I don't know where I think it should be directed.' Then you had seemed to change the subject to my relationship with my parents. Later I began to think: were you suggesting that when Quintana expresses this random anger she's directing it away from the people she is actually angry at? Meaning John and me?"

"Yes," he said. "Children get angry with their parents. If they don't grow up, they stay angry. But they can't afford to express it. Because they need your love and they don't feel secure they can't lose it."

I told him about Peggy Traylor calling me and telling me how upset Quintana had become when Susan said 'I hate you' to Peggy at dinner. Peggy had talked to Quintana about it and told her it was OK, but Quintana could not be calmed. Peggy said I had to tell Quintana it was OK to say I hate you. I saw her point, I agreed in theory. But I never did.

"Why not?"

"I don't know."

"I could tell you the generic reason – which is that you could never say that to your own parents – but it would be more useful if you thought about it."

I said that probably it had more to do with you. That if I were to tell Quintana it was OK to express anger, and she did, I would just get depressed and turn inside myself but you would express anger back and the whole thing would escalate, go out of control. I said that neither you nor I had grown up in families where the expression of anger was acceptable behavior.

"I only know what you tell me about John, but I'm quite sure you didn't."

I said I had in fact once written – inside a letter box — "I hate Daddy". It was the day he came home from Detroit at the end of the war. He brought presents. The whole day was very fraught. I was very moved by the present he brought me, because it was grown-up. Then we had lunch. There was a silver pitcher of iced tea. I was pouring from it when my hand slipped in the condensation and it dropped on the table. My father, who was very jumpy, reacted irritably. I ran into my room and locked the door. After a while he knocked but I wouldn't answer. And I wrote this on the inside of the box. So hard – with a soft pencil – I could never erase it. And finally I covered it over with address labels.

"You still feel guilty about it, don't you."

I said yes. Years later I burned the box.

"When I was in medical school, half the class was like me, entering early to get out early so we'd have doctors if the war lasted ten years. The other half was vets returning. They were older, a lot of them had families, and virtually every one of them reported an experience when a furious child said 'Why don't you just go back to the war.'"

24 May 2000

I remarked on the two-worlds effect in Fortune. The 21 year old
Stanford graduate who had turned down 5 "more desirable"
jobs to "intern" at Hewlett Packard for $75,000 a year, v. Robert
Bingham, who had recently died either a suicide or an OD,
and whose first book received on the same page of Fortune a
posthumous bad review.

He asked if I read stories about suicide.

I said I didn't make a special point of doing so, no.

"I wouldn't," he said. "You'll tend to dwell on it." He seemed to
muse. "Many children make dangerous choices," he said. "I have
a patient whose son wants to make documentary films. So she
gave him some very expensive equipment. And the first thing he
chose to document was a drug deal going down. Which could
have put him in real danger."

I said I often wondered – when I looked back on the dangerous
things I myself had done – how any children lived to adulthood.

"I wonder the same thing. I did dangerous things."

"And not just in the pursuit of so-called pleasure," I said. "I
don't mean just things like driving to Lake Tahoe late at night
drunk. I mean things I did even in the pursuit of experience, or
knowledge." I told him about walking into the surf at Stinson
Beach one night as a child – planning this, telling my mother
I was taking Jimmy to the Friday night folk dancing at the
Greyhound bus station, then leaving Jimmy at the bus station
and going to the beach with a notebook – just so I would know
how to describe it for a story I was writing about an ocean
suicide. And getting knocked down by a wave I couldn't see. "I
wasn't trying to kill myself," I said. "I was just trying to learn
something."

"I understand that," he said.

I told him about the two troubling dreams I had had about Quintana. In the first she was 11 or 12. You and I had been wrapped up in some dilemma of our own, and we had heard her opening a big box that had arrived but had not immediately looked into it. When I did go into her room, I saw the contents of the box neatly laid out – 18 school uniforms, 9 green jumpers and 9 yellow jumpers. In the dream, I had felt stricken, guilty that I had not taken care of the uniform question myself. Then I woke, and reasoned with myself that in fact I *had* taken care of the uniform question – always. Soothed, I went back to sleep – and immediately into an equally upsetting dream. In this one I was showing Quintana, now in her 20s, the Berkeley campus. I was very much the one in charge until I noticed, on the blackboard in a classroom, that she was to be the day's guest speaker. The class was in American foreign policy since 1945. I was seized by something near fear – Quintana, I thought, knows nothing about American foreign policy, what in the world is she going to talk about? I went to find you – you were somewhere else on the campus – and we went back to the classroom together. Then I woke up. Again I felt stricken, guilty, but this time I was awake. What I felt guilty about was that I had reflexively underestimated Quintana – maybe she knew things I didn't know she knew, maybe she was grown up. I was unable to shake this feeling – even though, practically speaking, I know for a fact she knows nothing about American foreign policy.

"You know they were both the same dream," he said. "They were both about the guilt you feel for having been – in your mind – remiss as a mother. You happen to be suffering from a depression. It's not a psychotic depression, because the guilt is not entirely unreasonable. You're not telling me you feel guilty for things you had nothing to do with, you're not telling me you caused the Holocaust, which is the kind of thing someone psychotically depressed might think. Your guilt is attached to reality. Something is wrong in Quintana's life. That's real, that's not a fantasy. Your depression, however, keeps you from seeing that fact as separate from yourself. You don't have a realistic idea of your role in this. Depressives tend to believe that they caused the problem, and they also believe the corollary – if they caused the problem, then they should be able to fix it. Sure, you may have made mistakes as a mother. Every parent alive makes mistakes with their children, and their children – most of them – live through it. What Quintana is going through is something you didn't cause. And you can't fix it. All you can hope for – all we're working toward here – is for the two of you to develop a closer relationship in the hope that this will ease the internal pressure she feels to drink, or escape."

I said that I had felt particularly helpless vis-à-vis Quintana at the wedding on Saturday. Everything had combined – the weather, the traffic, the interminable trip to and from, the lugubrious hymns, the rather joyless propriety of the occasion – to depress, and since I myself had felt in strong need of a drink by the time we got to the reception, I had been extra aware of what Quintana must be feeling.

"Did you find a way to say that to her? Make her understand that you had to be there, but she could congratulate everyone and slip out?"

No, I said.

"Why not?"

In the first place, I said, she really couldn't slip out, because it was seated, and the mother of the bride had called that morning to confirm that she was coming.

"But it didn't occur to you to convey to her that you sympathized with any discomfort she was feeling?"

I said I wouldn't have done that. Because I wouldn't have wanted her to jump to the conclusion that I thought she was in some way behaving badly.

"There are ways and ways to convey things."

I said that he knew how. He was trained to convey things. That was what he did. I on the other hand had trouble communicating – and when I tried I got it wrong.

"That sounds like your guilt talking again. What was her feeling about this event to begin with? Did she want to go or didn't she?"

I explained the chain of events, the invitation mixup. That when Lynn had called you and you had called Quintana, your impression had been that Quintana had felt hurt thinking she wasn't invited, and relief that she was.

"Did you talk to her about it yourself? Give her an out if she really didn't want to go?"

No, I said. In light of her expressed feeling that we were too much with her, we tried not to separately ask her the same question or make repetitive calls.

"I think absolutely you should be asking her things separately," he said. "That you should have a relationship with her and John should have a relationship with her. Separately. As well as the relationship you have with her together, which is different, and very valuable to her. But she needs the separate relationships. Children always feel that one or the other of their parents is the stronger, the one to whom they either can't say no or prefer not to say no. Daughters typically perceive the father as the stronger parent. In this case, it's no family secret that Quintana considers John the stronger parent. She talks to Dr. Kass about it. Which makes it especially important that she be able to express any concerns or doubts she has to you. Because she might not want John to think she has these concerns or doubts. This is a very normal kind of family relationship, but it's made acute in this case by two things: one, her situation, and two, your real fear of communicating. You were in the beginning extremely averse to communicating with me. You've become a good deal more open, although not entirely. If you could carry this openness into your relationship with Quintana, I think you'd see her reciprocating."

31 May 2000

I reminded Dr. MacKinnon that I would need a change of time the day of the annual meeting, and told him I had reduced Zoloft to a quarter tab every other day.

"As long as it does the job," he said.

I said I didn't know if it had been up to the job this week, since Quintana was back in Presbyterian for detox. I explained that last week we had been immensely encouraged, even made euphoric, by a couple of developments: I explained about her conversation with and about Griffin,* and also about Griffin's report that she had in fact been in touch with Robert Fox. These had seemed such good signs that both you and I had set aside, not mentioned to each other, certain danger signals on Sunday: a hint of having been drinking we each later acknowledged having picked up during a Sunday telephone call, her late arrival at Earl's Sunday night. Then the call Monday afternoon. Going down to her apartment. The extreme changeability of emotion. The hostility sometimes toward us, more expressively toward Dr. Kass.

"Why is she expressing hostility toward Dr. Kass?"

I said I assume that it was displaced hostility. That she was really mad at someone else, something else.

"She's angry at herself, yes. So she projects that anger onto everyone she's close to. But what form does her complaint about Dr. Kass take?"

I said she complained he didn't listen to her, wasn't interested in her, didn't care about her, etc. I had asked her if she had talked to him about this. She had said yes – although I wasn't sure she had – and that he had said "Everything I say or do has a therapeutic purpose." I said that there was a pronounced

* The actor, director, and producer Griffin Dunne is the son of John's brother Dominick.

irrationality on Monday about her complaints – I explained about the decision to keep her with us on Monday night rather than commit her to the locked psychiatric unit – she had been very much a part of this decision, both he and I had explained the choice to her and she had made it with us – but all evening she had railed at him for not hospitalizing her immediately – she was going to die tonight and nobody even cared – specifically Dr. Kass but implicitly us.

"But you were taking care of her. You were doing exactly what needed to be done. It was absolutely the correct decision not to put her in the locked unit, even though you must not have gotten much sleep that night."

I said she had quieted down considerably when Dr. Kass said it was OK to give her 20 mg Librium. That once she had taken the Librium it had evolved into a relatively quiet situation, she had even begun looking for an AA meeting. You had taken her to 73rd Street and then to 79th Street in search of one, and found that the next one was at 10 pm. So we had had dinner and I had gone to the meeting with her. I said that as he could imagine, a meeting at 10 pm on the last night of a big holiday weekend attracted some pretty hard-core cases, and she had seemed moved both by their talks and by their response to her. That she had begun crying silently during the meeting.

"What did you do when you noticed her crying?"

I said I put my arm around her.

"I have to tell you, I find this all very encouraging. She came to the two of you, the two of you responded, got her through it, made her see she wasn't alone."

I said that there was clearly still a good deal of alcohol in her blood. By the time we were on our way to the AA meeting, for example, she had forgotten she was going to the hospital in the morning, and when I reminded her she had in essence accused me and Dr. Kass of cooking this up behind her back. She had been extremely labile. She had lashed out at you, taken as a reprimand something you had said that was in no way intended as such. You had asked if she would prefer you left the room. She had snapped "Yes, leave." Then a few minutes later, it was "Where's Daddy, of course he's not here, he can't take it."

"No win," Dr. MacKinnon said.

I said that was what I had said to her. I had made a joke of it, said you can't have it both ways, you can't tell somebody to leave and then complain they're not here, I've read all the books, I know what this is, it's the kind of co-dependency game I'm not playing any more, count me out, I'm not playing. And – her lability was such – she laughed.

"You handled this very well. Really. More than very well. You said exactly the right things to her."

I said there was one subject that night on which she was entirely lucid, and extraordinarily direct. It had to do with her work, with photography. She said she couldn't bear to go through her photographs, it was just too painful, because when she went through them she knew that they were really, really good. I had asked why that was painful, and when she had seemed not to have a clear idea, had suggested that naturally it would be painful, and that the pain came from fearing that you would never find the will or nerve to show the work, to let it be appreciated. She had agreed. I said I had gotten a strong sense of how much easier it was for her to have a drink than to face her work. And a conviction that a lot of her current crisis came out of what might be called her career crisis.

"Absolutely it does," he said. "She drinks to medicate herself, to banish her fears about her future. I suspect that it's going to be crucial to her to find some artistic recognition. She needs to work, and to see her work appreciated."

I said she had talked earlier about something Robert Fox had said: that the alcoholic feels an emptiness inside, a hole. Drinking gives the impression at first of filling the hole – which is what makes it irresistible – and if you stop drinking you have to fill the hole some other way. AA fills it. That's the whole story of AA, he had told her, and it had seemed to resonate strongly with her. So I had at this point explained to Quintana that even people who weren't alcoholics felt that emptiness inside – anyone with the slightest tendency toward depression felt it – I felt it. Working was how I filled the hole. I reminded her that you and I always worked on weekends. I said we hadn't always done so. But at some point we had discovered that working through the weekend could allay what we had always called the Sunday jits. I had told her that there would come a time – I hoped – when she would find the same solace in work.

"The chairman of my department when I was a medical student used to say work was the most effective anti-depressant imaginable," he said. "That's why the catchword 'workaholic' actually has real meaning."

I said the fact that both you and I depended so heavily on our ability to work was part of what had made this past year so hard. This current crisis in particular seemed particularly hard.

"That's very interesting to me, because of everything you've just told me. Have you any thoughts about why it seemed particularly hard?"

I said I supposed it had to do with attrition, being worn down, not being able to find much immediate hope in this situation, given how many times we'd faced exactly the same thing.

"That could be one explanation, but another one occurs to me. I've watched you go through a number of these events – not all of them, but you've certainly described those that occurred before our first meeting. I would suggest that this one was harder on you because you allowed yourself to get closer to it. Closer to her. To intellectualize it less, to actually participate in her pain."

90

"You mean instead of trying to manage it, get past it, see the bright side and move on, wagons west?"

"That's exactly what I mean. I think you've been holding this at arm's length emotionally. Don't misunderstand me – I'm not suggesting you didn't love her. I'm suggesting that precisely because you loved her so much, you assumed for yourself the role of fixing it, making it all right. You're not doing that this time. You don't have any more answers. You're just feeling it with her, letting her lean on you. Which is what she needs. You can give her that now, because you've actually become a good deal stronger."

I said I thought the whole idea was for her not to lean on us, that part of her anger was that she was too dependent on us.

"She is, obviously. And she's going to have to grow out of it, if for no other reason than the obvious one, which is that unless she kills herself first, you and John are going to die before she does. But she needs to know you empathize with her – without trying to manage her – before she can grow out of it. Right now, what she needs is your uncritical, empathetic presence. Which is what you both gave her in this current crisis. It's a very draining thing to give. I know that. Doing what I do, dealing all week with patients who depend on me, when the weekend comes, I want to think about nothing. I don't want to see any cries and whispers movies. And when I talk to colleagues who do, I can't help but wonder if they're really listening to their patients during the week."

I said I had thought it might be a good idea – when Quintana comes out of the hospital – if she and I made a regular plan to go to a beginners' AA meeting together, ideally at a time when we could have lunch afterwards.

"That would be the best thing you could do for her."

7 June 2000
JDD, JGD*

Dr. MacKinnon said that he had prepared for this meeting
by talking at length to Dr. Kass. Dr. Kass now sees Q's basic
problem as one of her trying in every situation to please other
people. Dr. MacKinnon and Dr. Kass had discussed the problem
this presents in treatment – Quintana's tendency not to herself say
what's on her mind, but to wait for Dr. Kass to say something,
then try to please him by following that line, then to resent him
for not talking about what she wanted to talk about.

I said that something like this had come up over the weekend. I
had been talking to Q about ways people dealt with panic, allayed
anxiety. I did it by working for example. She had said that she
guessed for her what would allay anxiety was if she always did the
right thing and nobody got mad at her. This had seemed to me to
suggest a pretty clear problem.

"That's exactly what Dr. Kass was talking about," Dr. MacKinnon
said. "She tells people what she thinks they want to hear, then
resents them."

JGD said that last week, when she called us, he had tried to
get some basic information from her – our basic instinct being
reportorial – how long had she been drinking, was she going to
AA meetings. And that she had said "don't reprimand me," so he
had dropped it.

"She'll interpret any question as a reprimand," Dr. MacKinnon
said. "She'll interpret it as investigatorial, prosecutorial. This
is the first thing I always had to teach young doctors just out of
medical school. Everything about med school trained them to
ask questions, get the information. You can't get it by asking
questions of people in this kind of distress. A lot of the time they

* John Gregory Dunne (JGD) joined Didion (JDD) at this session.

92

can't even face the answer to what you're asking, no matter how elementary the question seems to you."

JGD said that I had gone to a couple of AA meetings with her on Sunday, and that she had asked if he were coming. He had said no. Then when he had later suggested going to a meeting with her, she had said "You said you didn't want to." But all JGD had been doing, he explained, was trying to follow through on the idea suggested by Dr. Kass that she saw the two of us as monolithic, always doing things as a unit.

"That's true," Dr. MacKinnon said, "but there are exceptions. You have to read her cues. Which can be very difficult to do, because this is so ingrained a part of her personality that she may not herself know what she really wants. The question of what she herself wants doesn't immediately occur to her, because she's so used to trying to do what she thinks you want. And then resenting you for it."

Dr. MacKinnon said that he had asked Dr. Kass if he were aware that there had been several close mother-and-daughter moments. Dr. Kass said that he was. Dr. MacKinnon had asked how Q felt about them. "She doesn't like them," Dr. Kass said. "But was she moved by them?" Dr. MacKinnon had asked. Dr. Kass had not explored this, which Dr. MacKinnon seemed to think an error. "Because of course she didn't like them," Dr. MacKinnon said. "She doesn't want to let anyone close, she wants to isolate herself, close the door and medicate herself. She doesn't want to be moved. But she has to be. So keep it up. The day you see her respond to tears in your eyes with tears in her own eyes, you know you've gotten somewhere."

JGD said that Quintana and I together had gotten rid of some bottles in her apartment. I said that I had asked her if there were any we should get rid of, and she had taken a vodka bottle from the freezer, then when I had asked her about a plastic bottle, she had smelled that and said yes, it was vodka. "Who poured it out?" he asked. I said that I had. "Why didn't you let her do it?" I said I was afraid it might be a trigger, it hadn't seemed a big thing, it wasn't as if we had different intentions. "You should have let her do it," he said. "These little things are important. You would have been granting her autonomy, independence to make her own decision." I said I was sure there were further decisions she could make on her own, because I hadn't asked her if there was anything in her bedroom. "Good," he said. "And don't delude yourself, she will go out and buy another bottle. Then she'll have to make the decision on her own."

Dr. MacKinnon said there was one area in particular that was very confusing to Q. This had to do with your and my relationship – which was in many ways unique, and had presented her as a very young child with a set of unique challenges. People who spend their entire lives together, he said, develop ways of living together – they provide each other space, they don't say everything they think at the moment they think it, they hold back from expressing themselves in ways that husbands and wives who lead more separate lives typically do not. "Your relationship remains extremely confusing to Quintana. She still has not one clue about how a relationship between a man and a woman actually works. She keeps trying to read you, and she can't. She imagines you want or expect things from her, but she has no idea what they are."

JGD brought up the question of the AA meeting Thursday night – would it be all right for him to go with her? "If she wants you to, yes." I said it would be hard to figure out what she wanted, since we would say "do you want it," and she would say "you don't have to."

"That would be an opportunity for you to address this question of her never saying what she herself wants. You say this of course not in a way she could interpret as reprimand, but in a way that shows you're all struggling with this together. You might say you've come to understand that you're part of what made her reticent about expressing herself, disinclined to say or even consider what she herself wants, but now you're trying to change that, break the old family dynamic. Take any opportunity you can to open this subject up, make her look at it, think about it, take the chance of saying what she wants even if she thinks it won't please you. If you could take one thing away from what we've talked about today, that would be the most valuable."

15 June 2000

Discussion of JDD's bad back (remedies for), discussion, initiated
by JDD, of way to gradually increase Zoloft dose to quarter-tab
daily. I said a quarter tab every other day wasn't really doing the
job, witness my mood yesterday.

Discussion of anxiety yesterday. I said a lot of it was about
work – our work life had seemed at least marginally under
control until Q's last hospitalization, but hadn't really seemed
in control since. And, because both of us had a big investment in
working, this spilled over into general anxiety. Which was one
reason I had thought it a good idea for you to join me last week.
I said we didn't really know where Quintana was emotionally.
Last Thursday night she had seemed pretty good, we had had a
good open discussion at dinner, you had gone to a meeting with
her, etc. This had carried over for a few days, then when I saw
her Sunday at St. John the Divine she had seemed emotionally
out of control, and had talked at the meeting in a way I had
heard her talk before, but only when she was in extreme
distress, drunk or coming off a period of drinking. I described
the meeting, her crying in the cathedral afterwards, then her
gradually coming out of it during the rest of the afternoon and
evening.

"She is in extreme distress," he said. "You have to realize, she's
still coming off a period of heavy drinking. It's still impossible
for her to maintain a steady state of mind. That's natural. All you
can do in this situation is be supportive, which you're doing. You
can't solve her problem for her. I think you should concentrate
on what she's doing right, the progress she's actually making. She
hasn't really done anything crazy or impulsively self-destructive.
She hasn't quit her job or taken a job she didn't want. She's really
exhibited remarkable patience with this, in a situation that would
make many alcoholics extremely impatient."

I said she had mentioned that Dr. Kass had told her that we were
afraid of her committing suicide. I said she had seemed surprised

by this, which had so confused me that my response had later seemed to me inadequate. I thought I had talked to her – that both of us had talked to her – several times about how devastated we would be. In retrospect, I could only think I had spoken too elliptically, that she hadn't gotten it.

"You probably did," he said. "Most people do. There's a kind of folk wisdom that you should never mention suicide to anyone who might be suicidal, that it could encourage them to do it. This simply isn't true. It's a myth, and a damaging one, because the one thing that might dissuade a potential suicide from carrying through with it is the sure knowledge that somebody he or she loves will be hurt by it. Suicidal people truly believe that the people they love will be better off without them. They need to keep hearing otherwise."

I said I was aware of that folk wisdom, and that it may well have colored the words I chose. I probably said "if anything ever happened to you", allowing her to think I was talking about a car accident. If I had said the word "suicide" at all it was probably in terms of how Stephen's suicide had affected the people who loved him, a parable, not necessarily directly related to her.

"Next time make it more direct," he said. "She gave you the opening. Use it."

I said that her apparent astonishment that this was a concern of ours had been particularly hard for me to understand because she herself had told me, in the New York Hospital E.R., that she had in fact – the night before we got back from Paris, when Tony and Rosemary* were staying with her – taken a lot of Librium after a lot of alcohol and had thought "I won't wake up in the morning, but Tony will find me."

"Did you point that out to her?"

---

* Tony Dunne is the son of John's oldest brother. He was married to Rosemary Breslin.

I said I hadn't. One reason I hadn't was that her blood alcohol that night at New York Hospital (we had later learned) was three-point something, so it seemed unlikely she would have any memory of telling me anything at all.

"Three-point something is extremely high," he said. "Which is another reason I think you should talk to her about this."

I said we had discussed the five-day weekend coming up.

"A killer," he said.

I said that was why we had brought it up. We had suggested she go to California, see her grandmother or see Stephanie or see Susan.* She had said that Susan had said come out and spend a month with me, but she, Quintana, didn't want to do it – Jesse would be there, the children would be there, all kinds of reasons not to go. I said this was an example of her misunderstanding of her friends. She had this conviction that she had no friends – but actually she did have friends, every one of whom she closed out, closed off. Which at some level she did recognize – but at another level she didn't.

"She doesn't think she deserves to have friends," he said. "She thinks she's offensive to them. That's her inner reality."

I said that after she seemed negative about going to Susan's, we had suggested Renewal at Hazelden. She had seemed to think this a very good idea, had called her Hazelden counselor Monday morning, and had developed and discussed with Dr. Boskin a fallback plan – Canyon Ranch – in case that didn't work out. I said I didn't know the outcome, but that she had seemed aware of the problem and anxious to avoid it.

"Whatever she decides to do," he said, "I'd revisit the idea of her spending some time with Susan and her husband and their children. In the first place, I think it would be good for her –

* Susan Traylor was a childhood friend of Quintana's. They went to school together in California and remained close.

maybe better than going to Hazelden, although you can't make that decision – to spend some time with healthy people. I'd just open up a discussion. 'What is it about Jesse and the children,' I'd say. 'Is it that you don't want to see them? Or is it a case of being afraid they don't want to see you?' I suspect she's afraid she'd somehow lay her problems on them – reveal herself as unworthy – that they'd get mad at her and want her to leave. In reality, that wouldn't happen – she's too civilized to let it happen – but in her inner reality, it's already happened."

I said we had spent a good afternoon with Susan and the children in April, that Quintana had been so wrapped up in playing with Pablo – her godchild – that I could hardly get her to leave before traffic time.

"Remind her of that. And use the word godchild. Every time you have an opportunity to stress that she's connected to people, seize it."

He asked if Quintana had been interested in the fact that you came with me for my appointment last week. I said I thought she was, that we had discussed it briefly at dinner, but that Quintana seemed to feel that however interested she might be, it was no one's business what got said to or by a psychiatrist.

"She doesn't want to intrude," he said. "But you could tell her that your talking about something that went on in one of our sessions doesn't mean you expect her to tell you what goes on in her sessions with Dr. Kass."

He asked if you thought our meeting last week had been useful. I said I thought so, yes.

"Did you discuss with Quintana what I had said about her not understanding your relationship?"

I said we had discussed it in the most general way.

"Maybe you should get into specifics. About what she doesn't understand. Because this is a deep part of her problem. She's still perceiving herself as part of a family dynamic that doesn't exist. If it ever did. If she were eight, and you were having the kind of conversations you're having now, you could set her straight in two weeks. But at her age, this kind of thinking can be very persistent. Correcting it – making her see her own misconceptions about herself vis-à-vis you and her father – is a central thrust of her therapy."

I said our discussion last week had made me think a great deal about how Quintana might as a young child have perceived us. I said I had seen a parallel to what Dr. MacKinnon had pointed out to me about the unspoken messages – my father's depression, his suicidal thinking, my mother's reaction to it – I myself had picked up as a child. In light of what I understood about myself, it seemed to me entirely possible that Quintana had picked up tensions in our own household – spoken or unspoken. I said that those years of her very young childhood were years when we had virtually no money, we were both worried, we had not been married long enough to be deeply committed to staying married. These were all perfectly natural tensions for that time in anybody's life or marriage, but Quintana may well have read them as potentially disastrous.

"Exactly. She knew she was adopted, she had these parents who had adopted her and loved her, but what would happen to her if something happened to them? I think you'll find that as she comes to realize how strong you really are, she'll begin seeing that this childhood reading was a bogeyman, a scary figment of her imagination."

I said I knew she had always thought of me as fragile.

"She does. I would imagine most people do. It's not just your physical fragility, it's the way you relate to people, the closeness of your emotion to the surface – everything about your emotional tone seems fragile. But you're not. You're really extremely strong."

I said a friend had once remarked that while most people she knew had very strong competent exteriors and were bowls of jelly inside, I was just the opposite.

"That's remarkably acute. If you've never told that to Quintana, I think you should. Preferably the next time you see her."

21 June 2000

Dr. MacKinnon asked me what I had been reading, what I had on my lap. I said it was something about revocable trusts I'd just taken off the net before I came. I said I was trying to gain ammunition for a call I was expecting from our lawyer. I said we wanted such a trust, for the obvious reason that it operates in lieu of any will and passes the assets directly without probate expense.

"Since the money saved would be from your lawyer's pocket, you can hardly expect him to show enthusiasm," he said.

I said that since he was in his eighties we expected to outlive him.

"But he has a firm. Probate is any firm's bread and butter. Who would you name trustee of the trust?"

I said I didn't know. That Quintana would be the beneficiary, and that a trust vesting in her would mean that when both of us died she would have, as I saw it, full control over it. I said there was an interesting thing about that. That even the last time we did a will I had tended to want to protect her by limiting her access to the assets. I no longer felt that way. Which seemed to me odd, since I now knew her to be in far less responsible shape than I had thought her when we last did a will.

"I don't think it's odd at all. I think it's an extremely healthy development. You realize you don't have control over her life. You're handing her the responsibility for her own life. These matters of inheritance are quite fraught. They're always about something more than the money. They force us to think about not existing anymore, to assess the success or failure of our lives. That's naturally a very emotional area. We try to skirt around it by discussing it in entirely legal terms, but it's still there."

I said I had gone through a great unspoken conflict with my brother at several points over our parents' wills. Specifically over the question of whether the trust they set up should vest in us or vest in our children. Obviously, a huge amount of estate tax would be avoided by passing our parents' estate through intact to our children. But I had opposed it, because it would mean that Quintana would get a quarter of the estate rather than the half she would get if the trust vested in me. I had prevailed in this, but it had been a continuing struggle, one we had never expressed out loud.

"That must have been very difficult. It must have brought all kinds of fears and apprehensions about family conflict, tearing the family apart. It might have even made you wonder about the value of the family."

I said that another fraught subject had come up yesterday, when I talked to my mother. She had asked my brother to buy a certain place to put her ashes. The church was only selling the places in twos, and Jim had said to me that it was an ideal time to move our father's ashes from where they were, his mother's family plot in Sacramento. I had been opposed to this, but had said only that we should talk it over with Mother. Mother, when I talked to her yesterday, was extremely opposed to it. She said the ashes were where he would have wanted them, she didn't want them moved. She had said this to Jim and then had thought she sounded terrible. I had told her I didn't think Jim understood either how strongly Daddy felt about Sacramento or how focused he was on his mother during the last year or two of his life. Mother had said she didn't think Daddy would have ever expressed that in front of Jim. I didn't think Jim would have heard him if he had. In any case, I had said I would talk to Jim. I knew it was going to be a battle.

"One that can't help touching on some examination of just how inseparable your mother and father actually were."

I said I might well perceive them as less inseparable than Jim. I had been more chronologically sentient during the war years they were apart. And I had been more keyed into the tensions of the postwar years. On reflection I saw that I did not really think of them as inseparable at all. I didn't think Mother did either. Yet since Daddy died I had several times – once when I took her to an event at Berkeley and his class joined the procession, a couple of times when somebody proposed a toast to him at a family event – seen her cry. Each time I had been a little surprised – and then I had thought maybe they were inseparable, never mind how unspeakable he was the last several years, she really misses him. Now I wondered if maybe it was more complicated than that.

"Tears are always more complicated than they seem. In my experience they can express almost any note in the scale of emotions. Your mother cries. You cry. If you explored the emotions behind your own tears, you might understand your mother's. Some people never cry. Their emotions are tamped way down deep. Yours are right there on the surface. I have the sense that your emotionality is one of the things that attracts your husband to you."

Not at all, I said. It irritates him.

"On one level, perhaps it does. On another, you've stayed married for 36 years, I can't think that's just lethargy."

I said that you were not one of those people who never cried, that I had in fact, although rarely, seen you cry. But it was always at an appropriate time. It wasn't over nothing. It was over, say, your brother dying.

"In my one brief meeting with him, I got a strong sense of a very good kind of stoicism, or control. I would say that he's able to deal with something and yet stand emotionally apart from it. And just as I would say that he was attracted to your emotionality, I'd say that you were attracted to his control."

I said that he had mentioned, last week, a certain surprise at my actual strength. I said I had been thinking about this, and had wondered if a lot of what looked like strength wasn't just a highly developed capacity to compartmentalize.

"You do compartmentalize, yes, but I see an actual strength."

I said I had then started thinking about where the capacity to compartmentalize came from. I said I thought it came from the basic way-west story that had been drummed into me as a child. You drop baggage, you jettison the piano and the books and your grandmother's rosewood chest, or you don't get to Independence Rock in time to make the Sierra before snowfall. I said I had come to see a lot of contradictions in this story, the principal one being, where were you when you got there? What did you actually have left?

"You know what this entire session has been about, don't you?"

No, I said.

"It's about being forced to sum up. Looking at your life. Asking yourself if you've truly lived it. Asking yourself what you've really got to leave behind. This is something everybody has to face. It's hard to face. But if you face it now, and make whatever changes you need to make, you're going to have a shot at dying peaceful."

I said I thought we were both feeling the pressure of time. Of not having time to do what was important to us. Of writing movies when we should be doing things we wanted to do. And that every time we thought maybe we had a shot at getting out from under our obligations – Quintana would kick in. And that sometimes I couldn't help feeling a certain resentment.

"Of course you do. You can't help but feel it. You feel imprisoned by responsibility for her. You're allowing her to hold you prisoner, which in turn imprisons her. She does feel imprisoned. She says so. She feels just as responsible for you and John as you feel for her. I think this realization of your resentment could have valuable consequences for her."

How, I asked.

"There's not a short answer. We have to think about it. We have to discuss it at length. But I think we're getting close to where we can discuss it."

28 June 2000

I said that it had occurred to me after we talked last week that the question we had gotten into – that of summing up your life, what it's been worth, what legacy are you leaving – had probably been on my mind all year. That the situation with Quintana had thrown into relief – and compounded – a more general concern about work, meaning, etc. That in fact this very question had precipitated what probably amounted to a late-life crisis.

"Very definitely," he said.

I said I recognized all that, but I still didn't know where to go with it, how to resolve it. I said the situation with Quintana was at the moment looking good. That she had responded very positively to the addiction specialist, that she identified with the group he had put her in and found it very useful. I said we could see the difference. She was looking better, of course, because she wasn't drinking, but she was also thinking better. She had even allowed herself to become extremely happy – and this was a worry in the back of my mind – about a dinner date she had had with someone. I said this was the first time we'd seen her this way in a long time – the worry of course was that it, or she, would crash.

"You could look at it that way, but there's another way to look at it. Obviously, she's making progress, she's allowing herself to hope, to make contact with someone outside herself. The very fact that she's exposing herself to possible disappointment shows great progress. There was a time – quite recent, too – when she wouldn't have risked that."

But what if it fails, I said.

"It might well fail," he said. "That's life. She's learning to live it. You could help her by enjoying it with her while it lasts – being optimistic. She can take something from your optimism. She can use it. It can make her more optimistic, give her ways of coping with her own depressive periods. You don't always have to look ahead for the bump in the road. Your anticipating the bump won't make the bump disappear. It'll still be there. You're afraid you won't be prepared to deal with it if you don't anticipate it, but you will. Your adrenalin kicks in. You deal with it. And meanwhile, you've been happy. Which gives you more strength to deal with it – and it also gives her more strength."

I said that after a lifetime of looking ahead to the bump in the road – or as I always thought of it, keeping the snake on cleared ground – I didn't see how I could stop now.

"People can change. I grew up in a family like yours, I was depressive like you, I was always looking for the bump or the snake. A lot of psychiatrists are attracted to the specialty because they themselves are depressed. That's why psychiatrists have a suicide rate four times the rate for other professionals. So I do know – from personal experience – that change is possible. Depression is a habit of mind. You can change the habit."

I said, vis-à-vis the effect of this habit of mind on Quintana, that we had mentioned to her this week that we were both depressed. This had seemed a source of considerable concern to her until we made clear that it had to do with a specific work problem. Which it didn't entirely, but we didn't tell her that.

"So long as you didn't let her think it had something to do with her. What was it about?"

I said it was about work, but more than any specific work. It had to do with where we were in our lives, wanting to do more work that was worthwhile and less that wasn't. I said that for many years we had been able to do pictures – a fair number of which got made – and still keep time to do what we wanted to do. This was increasingly hard to do. Some of it had to do with the economics of the picture business – more expensive movies, more development, more rewrites etc. A single picture could dominate years of our life and still never get made.

"At this stage in your life you clearly shouldn't be doing things you don't want to do. No one should. I for example had to make a decision not to treat patients I didn't want to treat. It meant making some sacrifices. I have no idea of your financial situation. Can you afford not to work?"

I said it wasn't a question of wanting not to work, it was a question of wanting to work on things that we did well, got some psychic reward for doing.

"So you'd still have income, but not as much income. Is that the situation?"

I said yes.

"Can you live on it?"

I said I had no idea.

"This is really very easy to figure out. I could tell you how to figure it out, I'm good at it, all my friends come to me when they have questions about money. But I'm sure you and John could figure it out by yourselves. You know what you have, you know what your income is likely to be for the year, you know what you'll spend."

I said there were two unknowable elements in that formula, what our income would be and what we would spend.

"You've never lived on a budget?"

I said no. I said we both assumed that we would probably have to cut back our spending. But by how much – or whether it was even a real factor – remained a mystery to me. We had made a stab at addressing the question last fall, I said. Maybe the most telling fault in our approach was that we had decided to address it in Paris, and taken the Concorde.

He laughed. "If the two of you are going to regain control of your lives, this would be the best possible way to start. I think you should sit down with your accountant, get a grasp on this."

I said obviously it was tied into our immediate legal dilemma.

"I think you better address that too," he said. "Because it's not going to get miraculously better. Obviously, you should be doing what you want to do. But you can't really do it until you get these questions about financial security resolved. That could well be one of the things that's worrisome or troubling to Quintana, too. Plus, it would be extremely useful to her to see you getting joy from your work."

I said she had seen it, but not recently. I said there were many things we should have done this year, and I wasn't even talking about books. I said you should have done the LAPD scandal, I should have done Miami.

"Yes. Definitely you should be doing these things. So figure this out, and do them."

I said there was another factor that could be standing in the way of that kind of reporting. I said that each of us had become exceedingly reluctant to go anywhere or do anything without the other.

"You're in each other's skin, yes. You get security from that, but it's also very limiting. This seems to be what makes Quintana sometimes feel herself to be an outsider in a family of two. Sometimes the two are keeping her out, in her view, and other times they're enveloping her, pressuring her. But it's two, and she's one."

I said I thought this two-ness had perhaps been reinforced – been increased exponentially – during and after the period when I was being treated for cancer and we didn't tell anyone.

"Yes, I think you're still showing scars from that. Scars you've never looked at. The physical scars healed but the emotional ones didn't."

I said I thought any scarring was not from the fact of having had cancer, but from the isolation.

"Have you told anyone since?"

I said we had told Calvin and Alice* at the five year point, and explained why we had felt particularly guilty about not telling them at the time.

"At the time you were being treated, didn't your doctors suggest you go to a support group?"

I said I never would have done that. In any case, I was *telling no one.* I even did the radiation at 168th Street so I wouldn't run into people I knew.

"I think we should get into this another time. Cancer still carries a heavy freight for many people."

I repeated: the freight for me wasn't the cancer, but it may have been the isolation.

"Whatever it was, I think we should get into it."

* Calvin Trillin and his wife, Alice, were longtime friends of the Didion/Dunnes.

5 July 2000

We talked about how successful Arizona had been for Quintana.
That she had played tennis every morning, taken care of herself,
got a real sense that she could in fact do things and take care of
herself outside a "treatment" context. How thrilled she had been
by the fireworks last night.

He said that it must have been a great relief to us to have the
sense that she was happy.

I said it had been. I said I had realized this morning – when I
realized that I had missed two months of B-12 shots – that I must
have been very very distracted, because this was something I did
religiously. Then when I looked back I saw that the first missed
shot had been during a non-hospital crisis with Quintana, and the
second had been missed when she was in Milstein for her third
round of detox.

"When there's a crisis, you focus entirely on the crisis. Which
usually means you focus on someone other than yourself."

I said we were actually able to engage in getting rid of the work
we had to finish before we could get on with what we wanted
to do.

He then initiated what seemed at first an irrelevant series of
questions about how a screenplay is written, how a scene is
worked out, how a character is developed. "You must have to
will yourself into the minds of these imaginary characters," he
said. I said yes. "That would require real concentration," he said
then. "Which you've recently found difficult if not impossible to
sustain."

I said yes, that this had of course been part of our general
dissatisfaction with work. That of course it was related to
Quintana's situation.

I mentioned having read that Smithers was moving away from the so-called Minnesota model. That they regarded this move as a return to traditional medicine – in which, if a treatment plan isn't working, you change the treatment rather than blame the patient. That managed care was encouraging them in that direction, because the outcomes studies didn't show much success with the Minnesota model.

"I wouldn't put much faith in the outcomes studies done by managed care," he said.

On the other hand, I said, even Hazelden's own version of its success rate seemed to me pretty low.

"Alcohol addiction – any addiction, really – is extremely resistant to any kind of treatment. Some people do come through, but I don't think anybody really knows why."

I said I didn't want to harbor any false hopes, but it had seemed to me this weekend that maybe Quintana could come through. That she had even mentioned her natural family in a way that seemed free of anger or resentment or anxiety. "Kind of ironic I'm in Tucson and Dallas," she had said at one point, but it had seemed free of freight. Which it hadn't been from the time they first contacted her.* I said that there were a lot of ways in which that contact had locked into and exacerbated her drinking problem. Most urgently, it had exponentially increased her feelings of guilt and anxiety. But there was something else. She had discovered that virtually the entire family, with the exception of her sister, was alcoholic. It would be possible to see this as an excuse she had seized on, but I saw it as more a case of her saying all right, they say I'm one of them, then I'll be one of them.

"If you believed in a genetic factor in alcoholism, that would tend to support it."

* Quintana's biological sister contacted her with the help of a private investigator in 1998. The family lived in Texas.

On the other hand, I said, if you believed in an environmental factor in alcoholism, you could find support in the families she grew up with, our own. I said I didn't suppose there had ever been in her childhood an evening when alcohol was not being consumed. And there had never been a social occasion on which somebody didn't get drunk.

"Somebody, sure. But it wasn't necessarily you or her father. Children are very acute to those differences. They can pick out the drunk at a party, just entering the room to say goodnight. She wasn't seeing you every night at home drunk, was she."

I said no, but she did see me every night at home having a drink. I said it was particularly important to me when I was working. While I was getting dinner I looked over the pages and marked them up. A drink freed me to do this in a way I couldn't do sober – it gave me a little edge.

"That's not the way alcoholics drink. They don't drink for the edge, or the buzz, or the slight loosening of mood. They drink to get drunk. They want oblivion. Where the alcohol ends up taking them, however, is straight from anxiety to depression and anger. They don't enjoy the stops along the way. So they don't stop along the way."

I said I had thought more about our discussion of cancer last week. I had examined my feelings about it, and I was still unable to discern any particular damaging emotion I had experienced having to do with "cancer" as a concept.

"You must have experienced fear," he said.

No, I said. I really didn't. My initial reaction was that this was ridiculous, this can't be happening to me, because I've never even had breasts. The fact that I was labeled "high risk" – that I had been seeing oncologists since I was about 35, that my mother had in fact had it – had apparently failed to make any dent in my picture of myself as breast-free. I said at two moments – the first when I told you that the ultrasound looked positive, the second when I got the call with the pathology report – I had in fact reacted for about ten seconds with tears. But I think they were more because I was frustrated, something had escaped my control, this something was going to be seriously inconvenient, this something moreover could be disastrous to our livelihood. Once I realized that it could be solved without threat to our livelihood, it never again bothered me. Except in one way. I had come to think of the solution itself – the secrecy – as the only residual damage. It had tended to isolate me – and us – even further than we were from other people.

"You already felt isolated, didn't you."

To some degree, I said, I had always felt isolated. I had felt extremely isolated as a child. This had continued through the time I married you. Together, in California, although we were still isolated, we had to some degree – a degree that I found quite comforting, a good part of our life there – become members of a community. We did holidays with people, we took hams to the house when somebody died, we had a certain – although at a distance – role in the community. I said that I had missed this when we moved to New York. It might not have existed much longer in California anyway – the people we knew were in many cases dying or retreating, and unlike many people we knew our daughter didn't want to make her life in the community – but I did miss it. I said that you had pointed out that our oldest friends were in New York, and they were, but for 24 years they had been forging a community without us, and we had been in a different community. And suddenly we weren't exactly in either one.

"John didn't feel this as strongly as you did?"

I said I didn't think so.

"He was more self-sufficient, didn't need it as much?"

Or didn't want it, I said.

"More active than not needing it. Could be. This can be remedied, you know. I think this is something we should talk more about, because it involves the extreme interdependence you've had with Quintana."

12 July 2000

I said that, barring some dramatic emergency, we were going to Honolulu the 21st and returning August 2nd in the morning, so I would see him next week and the afternoon of the 2nd but not the Wednesday in between. He said the week of the 2nd was his last week in, he would be away the remainder of August.

I said that Quintana seemed, given that she had had a couple of potentially upsetting developments, very stable. I explained about Marian,* then about the broken date, which on its own was unimportant but given what had been her perilous state of mind could have been quite damaging. I said we had been gratified to see that she responded to both in a realistic and even way.

"Of course the job situation has a long-term potential for upsetting her world," he said. "That will more than likely require some guidance, but it's possible for her to see it as an opportunity. House Beautiful is all photographs. She now has a friend there she might not have had before."

I said she did recognize that potential. And she was doing an assignment for Elle Décor in Washington that she seemed to be looking forward to – I said we didn't know whether it was the trip to Arizona or what, but something seemed to have converged to make her think herself capable of going places and doing things, less an invalid, less in some punishing "recovery" – just as punishing in its way as (and always carrying the threat of) "relapse".

"That does sound promising. Will she be in Washington while you're away?"

I said she would be in Washington the first weekend we were away, and that we planned to ask a friend to ask her to the

* The editor Marian McEvoy moved from *Elle Decor,* where Quintana was working as a photographer, to *House Beautiful* on July 6, 2000.

country the second weekend. So – if she was at loose ends or worried – she would have somewhere to go.

Change of subject. I said that last Wednesday evening, after the discussion we had Wednesday afternoon about cancer and not telling and isolation, it so happened that we were having dinner with someone who had herself had breast cancer a year after I did. She had not kept it secret – even if she had wanted to, it would have been difficult, since she required chemotherapy. A year or so after her treatment she and I had had a series of what had seemed to me – for two people who were not best friends – extraordinarily open conversations about how having cancer had affected her. It had occurred to me at the time that I wanted to tell her about my own cancer, but of course I hadn't – for one thing the conversations occurred in an out-of-time situation, in the atrium at McKeen when her mother-in-law was dying and you were hospitalized for arrythmia. Time had passed, and I had not again had the impulse, but Wednesday night, when she and her husband disclosed that she had been undergoing recurrence – of a grave kind, liver – and had told very few people, I again felt the impulse, very strongly, and told them. It had been a liberating but in many ways a frightening thing to do. Then she had called. I described her call and the word she used: "translucent."

"You were open with her – in other words you gave her something – and she gave you something back, she was open with you."

I said possibly being open came more naturally to her because she was the daughter of two psychiatrists.

"It doesn't work that way. In fact the common joke among psychiatrists is that we have the most messed up children of all."

I said that Carolyn had in fact intimated that growing up with psychiatrists hadn't been easy, that she had always felt that she was being watched and not living up to what was expected of her.

But of course, I added, what middle class child doesn't feel that way, no matter what his or her parents do.

"Every one of us feels that way growing up. The question is whether and at what point and at what cost you get over feeling that way."

I said I doubted that I would have been open had he and I not been talking about it only a few hours before.

"I'm sure that's true. But the point is, you were. Do you think you could be open enough to tell Quintana about these conversations with her?"

I said that we had in fact told Quintana, but I had no idea how much she took away from the discussion – that she had not responded as if she found it as remarkable as we did.

"Never mind what she said or didn't say. Believe me, her unconscious has to have taken something very valuable from that discussion. You were telling her – whether you knew it or not, and whether she recognized it or not in her conscious mind – that she didn't have to be totally responsible for you, that you're not totally dependent on her, that she's not your prisoner. That you have a life independent of her, you have friends, that you talk to them, that they respond to your talking to them. It's not all on her. When you and I started talking, we were focused narrowly on how you could deal more effectively with her. Then, necessarily, our discussions got wider. We've been talking about how you could deal more effectively with other people in your life, deal more effectively with your life itself. These are wider questions, but they can't help impacting how you and Quintana deal with each other. I think this is an example of that."

I said I recognized that the emotional isolation we had discussed could have tended naturally to make me over-dependent on her – in the sense of being too emotionally invested in her. I said it was weird to me – a little ironic – to now think of myself as having been too close to her, when the conventional guilt trip for mothers absorbed in their own work or lives is that they aren't close enough.

"You dismiss that kind of guilt as conventional, but it would have been difficult for a woman as busy as you were not to have – at one point or another – felt it. And possibly overcompensated."

I said it had occurred to us that she was too close to us, but it had never occurred to me that I was too close to her. Particularly at the time of her adolescence. My mother once said that if she had raising children to do over again, she would have sent me away from the time I was 12 until the time I was 20.

"There's typically a good deal of stress between adolescent daughters and their mothers. They have to push the mothers out of their lives. They have to make sure they're dead. Then they feel guilty about it. Sometimes the stress is such – partly because it has to do with sex, and that's unmentionable – that mothers and daughters never reestablish real openness or closeness."

I said this had been true in the case of my mother and me, but that I had tried to avoid the flash points with Quintana. In a lot of potentially stressful situations – chaperoning parties, shopping for clothes – I had been able to substitute Dominique for me. Which had been very, very successful. Dominique was only 6 years older than Quintana, and Quintana adored her, even idolized her. I had found myself wondering this year if Quintana would have been in quite as dire a situation as she was if Dominique was still alive.

A silence. "What are you thinking about right now," Dr. MacKinnon asked.

I said I was thinking about Dominique. I had so many times regretted not talking to her. The boyfriend had always given off bad vibrations. Dominique's mother felt them, and let Dominique know she didn't like him, which infuriated Dominique, and at least at the beginning I hadn't wanted to fall into the role of another obstructive mother in her life. But it began to be clear she wasn't happy. She was drinking too much, she was overanimated, she had the flush of unhappiness. I could have talked to her. I'd talked to her about other things, for example not using abortion as birth control. And after we ran into her father in New York and he said she'd been beaten up and had broken up with the boyfriend, I had resolved to talk to her, to tell her the danger of letting him back into her life. But things came up, the opportunity didn't immediately present itself. And the next thing I knew she was dead.

I explained the circumstances of her death.

"What do you imagine you could have ever said to her that would have prevented that?"

I said I didn't know. But we were close. I should have tried.

"Did she change her behavior after you talked to her about abortion?"

I said I doubted it.

"Sorrow is one thing. Guilt is another. Obviously, she should never have gone outside onto that driveway. She'd been beaten up at least once before, probably more. There's a kind of dangerous behavior that defies the best attempts of caring people to prevent it."

I asked if he meant dangerous behavior on her part.

"Obviously. She was behaving dangerously. You see it in abused women again and again. There's a dangerous level of grandiose thinking. They think they can handle the situation, make him better. They never can."

I said I supposed there was a level of grandiose thinking on my own part. To think that I could have prevented it. Solved her life. Like thinking I should be able to solve Quintana's life.

"My point exactly."

6 September 2000

Dr. MacKinnon asked how my August had been. I said that I had been trying to write something about the campaign, and had quite a bit of trouble getting into it – even concentrating enough to think at all, or read the books without going to sleep. And that you had been having a similar problem with a novel. In the past week, however, I had been able to concentrate – and you had worked through the immediate problem with the novel. And I realized it was at least partly because Quintana was in Arizona.

"You didn't have to be responsible," he said. "You couldn't watch her."

I said yes, that was certainly part of it. And in my case there was something else. The very subject I had finally decided to write about kept bringing up questions of "faith". Which had brought to mind my own lack of it. As well as my own feelings about AA, and the whole question of "faith" in the program, and the difficulty Quintana seemed to have with it. My problem, I said, was that I understood the difficulty.

"My own sense," he said, "is that whatever success or lack of success Quintana has with her drinking problem doesn't turn on this question."

"You think it turns instead on whether she actually wants to stop," I said.

"Whether she's capable of making that commitment," he said. "Absolutely. The whole twelve-step process – they're not bad ways to live, they won't hurt you – is just a way of reinforcing or supporting that initial commitment. Giving the alcoholic a positive program to fill the space that drinking filled. It's not magic. It won't make the commitment for you. When you hear someone resist AA in a strong way – and the most typical line of resistance has to do with 'all that God business' – you have to look for the reason they're resisting. And in one or another version, it always comes down to their not being ready to give up the support they get from drinking."

I said that August had been difficult for her. She had been getting quite a bit of support from Dr. Roscan's group, but of course it had disbanded for August. Dr. Kass was away. Her best friend had moved to Las Vegas. Her job situation had deteriorated dramatically, to a point about ten days ago, a Monday, when she simply did not go to work. When we talked to her on the phone that day she had not been drunk, but she had exhibited the emotional lability and fragility that we had come to associate with her drinking.

I said that this one phone call had immediately plunged us both into despair. We didn't at that moment see any end to the problem. We weren't hearing from her anything that indicated a determination to come out of this OK. There was, at that point, no way even to talk to her about it. All we wanted was to get her out of town in one piece. We knew she'd be better once she was at a physical remove from the office. And yet, even in Arizona, she didn't seem – at least the one time we talked about it – to have a stable view of her situation. She was like a child. She kept saying "But Peggy will get all mad at me." And there was no way of getting through. "What difference does it make," we would say, "you're planning to leave anyway." And she would agree. Then it would begin all over again: Peggy would be all mad at her.

"Clearly, she can't bear to have anybody mad at her," he said. "She has given over her approval of herself entirely to other people."

Obviously, I said. But what to do about it? Dr. Kass talks to her about being more assertive. She knows it's an OK thing to be assertive. But she can't be. I tried to talk to her about this, before she went to Arizona. What's the problem with asserting yourself, I said. She said Dr. Kass thought it must have something to do with not feeling she could assert herself as a child, that perhaps you or I or both of us had discouraged it. And I said, well, maybe we did, but we're not doing it now.

"No," he said. "But she can't get that picture out of her head. She's still looking at this from a child's point of view. This is what adolescent rebellion is all about, this is the purpose, you get the old pictures out of your head. She didn't do that."

I said I had this week had a certain insight into the way I might have treated her as a child. I told him about thinking, when I heard that Nat Rich had hemorrhaged after a tonsillectomy, that he must have cried too much. Immediately I realized that this was why I thought you and I and Stephen had hemorrhaged: I had cried, it was my fault. I was four or five when this happened but it was still the picture I had of it.

"Somebody put that picture into your head," he said.

Or I thought it up myself, I said.

"Based on previous experience," he said.

I continued. A few days after realizing this, I had been talking to Mother and told her that Quintana would probably be changing jobs, her current one had become with the new regime not a productive situation at all. Mother's immediate reaction was "Of course she takes so much time off."

"In other words it was her fault, just like hemorrhaging was your fault. I understand this pattern all too well, I grew up with it. It's the way Protestants bring up children. In the interests of promoting modesty in children – a Christian virtue – they massacre self-esteem. It's always the child's fault. Because if it wasn't the child's fault it would be their fault. Everything has to be somebody's fault in this scheme. There are no accidents. When I hurt my leg this winter, naturally I blamed myself. I was talking about it to a colleague one day, another psychiatrist, a Jew. And he looked at me and said 'You guys really won't let yourselves believe in accidents, will you.' It's a way of bringing up children that can only end in one of two ways, rebellion – that's the usual way – or overdependence. And when you match an over-dependent grown child against an overprotective parent, you reach a kind of stalemate."

I said I knew that I had been physically overprotective of her. She was as a very young child physically fearless, and I had made her so afraid of the water that she had a slow time learning to swim. I was so afraid something would happen to her.

"I wonder if this extreme fear that something would happen to her might not have had something to do with your feeling a certain guilt that she didn't have your full focus every second of every day. I don't know exactly where you got that guilt, but I know from things you've said that it's there. To be a parent, you know, doesn't necessarily mean to have the child in your eyeline every second of every day. That's not what it's about. Was there anything like that in the way you were brought up?"

I said it was very possible that there had been. I said that I had noticed, when Quintana was small and I took her to Sacramento, that all attention was focused on her. All conversation was directed to her. No one talked directly to anyone else.

"They did talk to each other, but they talked through the child."

Yes, I said. And I suppose it had been the same when I was a child. Even the way the chairs in our living room were arranged supported this arrangement. Daddy insisted that all chairs and tables be against walls. So there were four walls lined with furniture, and a big space in the middle. Preferably with a child in it.

"That would have been a very curious way to grow up. Everyone talking to you, but not really to you. I wonder if this isn't why you have almost no concept, today, of direct conversation. You talk directly to me now, but you certainly didn't when you first met me."

I said it hadn't been my experience that people talked directly. I said that I did however find this thing interesting. The thing about the abnormal focus my family – particularly my father – placed on children. I knew – once I was an adult – it was abnormal. One reason I knew it was because you pointed it out to me. But maybe it was still there in my mind as the way I should be focused on Quintana.

"And it has some bearing, I would think, on the mixed feelings you have now. The guilt. And the resentment."

13 September 2000

I said that we had had dinner with Quintana Saturday night.
That she had gotten back Thursday, gone to work and seen
Dr. Kass on Friday, and when I talked to her on the phone had
seemed to agree with Dr. Kass that she should wait at least two
weeks before quitting, get her next moves lined up. On Saturday
night, however, the "get her next moves lined up" part had
vanished from the equation. The message instead was that work
was such "hell" that she could do nothing except count the days
until she quit. I said that we had found this discouraging. That
I had probably read the evening as more discouraging than you
did – you had thought she was fine at first, then had suddenly
turned negative.

I said you and I had discussed the question of financial support
the next day. And had agreed with his suggestion that we do it as
a lump sum, a certain amount of money that she would otherwise
inherit but that could help her more now.

"Good. You might think of it as tuition. Tuition in life."

I said I had to admit that to some degree it was making me mad –
not the money – but having to worry about what would happen
when the tuition ran out.

"You're anticipating the worst again. Don't. She'll spend money
on something foolish, sure, but then she'll learn to allot it where
she needs it."

I said it had seemed to me this week that she was handing over
the full responsibility for what happened to her to us – and
perhaps alternately – when she was with him – to Dr. Kass.

"Of course she is," he said. "And the reverse of the coin is that
you're accepting it."

I said I wasn't accepting it. That was what I was just realizing.

"Yes you are," he said. "Maybe not all the time, but at least some of the time. Some of the time you're accepting it and maybe at other times John is accepting it. Because every time you feel guilty about her – every time you feel responsible in some way for what is or isn't happening to her – you're letting her turn over her own responsibility to you. I know perfectly well that there are a significant number of hours in every week that you or John or both of you spend worrying about her. This isn't some special insight on my part, I'd be very surprised if all of your friends didn't know it too. Most importantly, she knows it."

I said that last week he and I had talked about her extreme fear of people "getting mad at her", which she believed went back to her childhood fear of you or I getting mad at her. About how she couldn't seem to get beyond this childhood interpretation. She was always in her mind the "victim" of other people. I said I knew that she and Dr. Kass had talked about this sense of victimization – the only way I knew it was that sometimes when she was in a good mood she would make a joke about it: like "there I go again, I'm the victim." This week it had occurred to me that the reason she couldn't get beyond this – couldn't in effect grow up – was that she was getting some psychic gain from it.

"Of course she is," he said. "It allows her to blame you. And every time you accept responsibility for her, she can blame you further. Whatever happens to her has to be your fault, since you made the decisions, you were supposed to protect her, she's your responsibility. Little children don't worry about themselves, because they expect their parents to protect them. Part of growing up is realizing that your parents can't always protect you. She doesn't want to cross that bridge."

I asked how we could help make her cross it.

"Stop worrying about her so much. She presents a kind of decision-making vacuum. The natural impulse is to enter it –

make the decisions for her – but don't. And make sure that she knows you're not worrying so much about her. Make her start taking a few steps on her own. Don't anticipate the mistakes – although I know that's your makeup. So she makes a wrong decision. Don't expect it to be the end of the world. Say she does make a mistake. And say she says to you, why didn't you warn me, why didn't you stop me. Don't backtrack and feel guilty at that point. It's a major chance for a learning experience. Tell her you don't have all the answers, tell her that her own judgment is as good as yours, let her know you're not trying to protect her because you know you can't always protect her."

I said that last week he had suggested that I had overprotected her because I had at some level felt guilty about not giving her my full focus, that at some level I had had a peculiar idea of what being a parent should involve. I said this had surprised me, because as I had frequently told him I never felt in the least guilty about working.

"I told you last week, I was never talking about your working. There was something else you felt you weren't giving her."

I said that my mother and father had each in their different ways made clear that they thought I was a less than appropriately devoted parent, out too much, relied too much on help, not enough hands-on attention etc. I said, however, that I never thought this got to me, because my parents had long since lost their ability to make me feel guilty.

"They pretty much wore it out, would be my guess. But some of it still gets through."

I asked if he meant I had over-protected her not just because I was afraid of losing her but because it would certify me to myself as an adequate parent.

"I certainly think guilt was a big component in your parenting strategy."

I said I did know that I had felt guilty about little things (school open houses, Christmas pageants, etc etc etc) that didn't bother you in the least.

"That's what Dr. Kass thinks. Based on what Quintana tells him. She doesn't read John as having over-protected her. It's you. So she gets mad at you for over-protecting her and mad at John for not."

I asked how she could be mad at you for not.

"She thinks he got mad at her more than you did. Shorter fuse."

I said you had temperamentally had a shorter fuse. You got mad and expressed it, I got mad and withdrew. That was how we were wired.

"That's how most families are wired. What was your attitude if he got mad at her? The instinctive thing, and it's the wrong thing, is for the mother to step in to defend the child."

I said I supposed that that had been my instinct.

"That's what mothers do on wildlife shows. We're more evolved now. There's a very fine line here. It's a hard line to walk. Naturally, the mother's instinct is to want to convey empathy to her baby, let her know she's not alone, that she, the mother, will protect her. But the baby, who misconceives the father's temporary anger as dangerous, reads the mother's defense as agreement with this misconception: there's a danger here, without me you'd be helpless. The most successful dynamic is when the mother manages to convey something light, something along the lines of 'look, you know his moods, it'll pass,' in other words letting the child know there's no danger. You should have been able to manage that, you had a father you could rely on."

I asked if he meant my own father.

"My impression is that you could rely on your own father, yes."

I said yes, I could. As a child I had thought he was mad at me all the time too, and it had made me mad, but it hadn't seemed to have a long-term effect. Although my mother had much later told me that after World War Two she had wanted a divorce, and the reason she wanted a divorce was that he had during that period been so constantly in a rage with my brother and me. He used to tell her, she told me, that I deliberately left drawers open just to make him angry.

"That was a very rough period for a lot of families. The reunion didn't go easily."

I said it hadn't gone easily at all in my family, partly because we were living with my grandmother.

"A lot of men came home and felt they no longer had a place in their family."

I said I thought it had been very hard for Daddy. He had a depressive tendency to begin with. He came home into a situation that was totally designed to have no place for him. My grandmother and my grandfather basically lived apart. So there was this little self-contained world of women and children, humming along without him. And my mother could not have been an easy person for him to deal with. She was embarrassed by any display of affection. She didn't like to be touched. She told me much later that she had "never liked that part of marriage", by which she meant sex. I remember right after the war Daddy bought her a hat, a very glamourous movie-star kind of hat, big brim, lacy black veiling. She returned it to the shop.

"I hope we can continue with this next week. Once you start trying to understand how your own parents felt – and how you felt about it – you've gone a long way toward understanding where you are with your own children."

20 September 2000

We talked first about dinner with Quintana Monday night, which she had said was to "discuss my plan". I said that both of us had had a sense of foreboding about how to handle this dinner, since our previous discussion of her plan had seemed fruitless. Sunday night we each had dreamed about it – you about how to handle it, me about having a small child given into my care who was suddenly, inexplicably, and overwhelmingly in a rage at me.

At some point Monday, I said, exhausted by the prospect of dinner, we had talked about how to handle it and decided in effect not to handle it. To do what he and I had talked about. Just to listen. To take the approach that everything was going to work out well. We had done this. And it had worked: she told us she intended to quit on Friday and we had said we thought that was a good plan. And then we talked about how best to implement this, without getting into her further plans. We had tried to convey the simple sense that we were wholeheartedly behind her, and her response both that night and since had been positive.

As it turned out, I said, she ended up quitting yesterday, because Peggy Russell had turned the screw yet again. First her office had been taken away, then her photography assignments, then her assistant. Now she was told that the new assistant she had been told to hire and train wouldn't even be hers, but the art director's. Then Peggy had said you don't seem happy, and Quintana had said no, she wasn't, and she quit. Obviously, I said, Peggy was trying to get her to quit.

"She would have been much better off financially if she'd made this woman fire her," he said.

I said that this was the very point on which our previous dinner had foundered. We had urged this, and she simply couldn't seem to get it. I said she didn't know how to play these games.

"Obviously," he said, "she was approaching it in terms of her own ego. She didn't think she could withstand the assault to her ego of being fired. It would make her feel too bad."

I said in fact both Dr. Kass and we – at a point during the past year when she was hospitalized and wanted to tell Marian to fire her – had told her not to, that it would make her "feel too bad".

"At some level she still thinks that," he said. "But she also knows that in this new situation they *wanted* to fire her. So she still feels bad. The worst of both worlds. She feels she got fired, but she did herself out of the benefits of being fired. How do you feel? I have the sense you wish you'd been able to talk her into playing the game the smart way."

I said that naturally I did.

"And you feel guilty that you couldn't. Why do you feel guilty?"

I said I felt guilty because I had failed to teach her how to be smart at this kind of thing. Among other things I had failed to teach her.

"I don't know how you could teach her what you don't know yourself," he said.

I said I did know it myself. I might not have known it when I was in my 20s – in fact I didn't, I never played the smart game at Vogue and I didn't care – but if there was one thing working in the movie business had taught me, it was how to play hardball.

"Give me an example," he said.

I told him about our "Star Is Born" exit.*

* Didion and Dunne wrote the first three drafts of what became the script of the 1976 version of *A Star Is Born,* the one starring Barbra Streisand. Other writers worked on the film after they exited the project, but Didion and Dunne retained credit and a share in music and record royalties. Streisand won an Oscar for Best Song ("Evergreen") and the soundtrack sold more than 8 million copies worldwide.

"You have situations like that, you have a lawyer guiding you through them. She doesn't. More importantly, you have layers of lawyers and agents between you and the situation. You don't have to go into an office every day by yourself and play a role. You play hardball at a very protected remove. I doubt very much you could negotiate this kind of situation face to face. You're not a negotiator. You rather spectacularly lack the skills for dealing with other people. You're afraid of them. Not unlike Quintana. In your case you solve the problem by steering clear of them. She hasn't been in a position to do that."

I allowed that this was true.

"That you don't know how to negotiate isn't your fault. People learn to negotiate as infants. Tiny children. Or they don't. They learn to negotiate by negotiating with their parents. Or, they accept their parents as unnegotiable, all-powerful. They acquiesce. They may resent it, but they do what their parents want them to do without questioning it. They even anticipate what their parents want."

I said that negotiation between Quintana and us had not been part of the equation.

"How could it have been? You weren't brought up to negotiate. Neither I would guess was John. Naturally, you brought up your own child the same way. These patterns go back for generations. Quite often there comes a point when children who don't know how to negotiate decide they can no longer afford to meet those anticipated expectations. They still don't negotiate. They don't know how. Their pattern at that point is to walk away, close the door. From everything you've told me, that's what you did. And still do. I'm trying to tell you not to be so hard on yourself. Anything you failed to teach Quintana was something somebody failed to teach you. You're not all powerful. Neither were your parents. You can't teach somebody what you don't know."

I said that our next dinner with her was being framed as a celebration. I hoped we would get some sense from her about what her next steps would be, but we weren't going to ask.

"Don't ask. No. And if she says 'what do you think I should do next,' don't take that opportunity to tell her. Say you have no way of knowing what she should do next. All you know is what you should do next, and that's listen to her. She knows the world she's in, she knows what she wants. Also, I think it could be valuable to her if you told her that you completely understand why she chose to have the sense of control that quitting gave her. You understand that getting fired would have meant to her a loss of control, any possible benefits to one side. That would be a way to teach her something without her realizing that she's being taught. It might occur to her down the line that there might have been benefits in not cutting off her nose to spite her face, that she might be better off in the future negotiating these things. When children get to be her age you have to teach them things in this very backhanded way, but you can still teach them. I sometimes think one of my few successes with my daughter was backhanded. I was helping her with some advanced algebra assignment, and she asked me a question I simply couldn't answer. So to cover myself I said 'let's go back a few pages.' Just stalling. Lo and behold, while I was stalling she came up with the answer herself, and thought I was very smart for having led her to it."

I said my own efforts to help Quintana with her homework – which were extensive – were probably in retrospect too based on taking it over, showing her how to do it rather than prompting her to discover herself how to do it.

"Teaching is something very few parents can do. There's this fad now for teaching children at home. I have no idea how they do it. Moreover, it's a terrible idea, because a certain amount of schooling is about the development of social skills."

I said I thought that one reason my own social skills were underdeveloped was that I had gone to a lot of different schools as a child, and some years not gone at all. So I was always the new girl, outside and in each instance at first a little behind.

"That's very traumatic."

I said I didn't consider it a trauma, but it had been a definite factor.

"It is a trauma. You go through serial periods of not having friends, not being invited. That's traumatic to a child. Unless the child is already so traumatized that he or she just closes it off. I don't think parents realize this."

I said that my own parents had dealt with it in a way that only intensified my non-acquisition of social skills – by suggesting that friendship was worthless, that I was better than anyone I wanted to be friends with.

Which brought up, I said, something I wanted to ask him. Last week he had said that it was valuable to try to understand the point of view of one's parents.

"To see where your own point of view came from, yes."

Did he mean, I asked, that when you come to understand your parents, you understand the demands you thought they placed on you, and in effect "forgive" them? And that's the point at which you emotionally grow up?

"That's the point at which you become an integrated person, yes. The point at which you no longer feel guilty about not meeting whatever you imagined your parents' expectations to be. And, further, the point at which you no longer feel guilty about how you did or did not fail your children. You started seeing me at a crisis in your life. The crisis had to do with your relationship with your child. You were sent to see me because I understand the kind of crisis you were in and also because I'm older. You could never have talked to a younger psychiatrist. You would have sensed that he or she lacked the experience you've had. Young people do very well with young psychiatrists. People like you don't. All we've been trying to do here is get you to a point where you don't feel that guilt. You and Quintana had been for too long two people in the same skin. You read any failure on her part as a failure on your part. That was too heavy a burden for you to bear. And bearing this responsibility for your happiness was too heavy a burden for her to bear."

I said that sometime in the past week I had a dream about being at the Broadmoor with Quintana and she was drinking. The dream wasn't the point. The point was that when I woke up, I started thinking, and realized that I had been dreaming about Quintana being drunk or OD-ing since she was a child. When it wasn't an issue. It made me wonder if this tendency to always anticipate the worst outcome had been in Quintana's case self-fulfilling.

"No. You did not wish or will her into the situation in which she found herself this past year. You didn't do it, you can't control it. But it would be interesting to find out where those dreams did come from."

I said that I had thought a great deal about the point he brought up last week, which came down to my expecting or wanting Q to be able to do things I couldn't do myself – to be in effect the me I couldn't be. This had interested me on a lot of levels. On the first level, we all know parents whose aspirations for themselves seem to depend on their children's performance – the extreme emphasis on "getting into Harvard" being the most obvious example. I had always been extremely disdainful of this, had even taken pride in not doing it myself. We just hadn't done it, either of us. That kind of performance wasn't important to us. But on another level, obviously I had done it – not in those obvious ways, but done it nonetheless. I had even been aware at some level I was doing it – I can remember thinking, how wonderful, she's adopted, she's not carrying my limitations, she can be anything she and we want her to be.

Then, I said, I had thought further about this. It had occurred to me that, if in fact I had been asking her to be the person I couldn't be, I had been doing to her exactly what my father did to me. One of the big ordeals of my childhood was visiting relatives with my father, which we did all the time. This was particularly painful when we visited his mother's family, which had a very gregarious, noisy style. Somebody was always sitting down at the piano and singing, performing. Lots of jokes. The cousin on that side nearest to me in age was always described approvingly as "a real firecracker", or "that Patsy, she's a pistol." I on the other hand was extremely shy, very withdrawn at the best of times, and exposure to this family would render me almost paralyzed. I could barely speak. Which would infuriate my father. The drive to and from my aunt's house was always an agony, instructions and warnings en route and recriminations on the way home. Why couldn't I respond. Why couldn't I be more like Patsy. Look at Patsy, she can handle a joke. My mother had always said at the time, "I don't understand why he wants you to be that way, he's not that way himself", but I had never until this week entirely put it together. He himself was extremely shy. He himself was withdrawn. And yet at the time his mother died he had been taken in by this family. They more or less raised him. And to some extent he must have always felt the same way I did.

"And he always felt an outsider," Dr. MacKinnon said. "He didn't want you to be one. Shyness is inherited, you know. My colleagues who work in that area have demonstrated that shyness exists or doesn't exist in the first few hours of life. Touch a shy baby, the baby flinches, or withdraws. It's in the neurological wiring. They absolutely inherit it."

Then how did Quintana inherit it, I asked.

"In the first place, you have no way of knowing what she inherited. In the second place, if you take care of a child from birth, a certain amount of your own wiring gets wired into the infant. Babies are born with genetic tendencies, but their early environment goes into determining their ultimate development. There's a certain area in which you can't tell the difference."

But here's the other thing, I said. Going back. If that's what I was doing vis-a-vis Quintana, was I transmitting to her the same sense of disappointment that my father transmitted to me?

"If you were, you couldn't help it. You weren't doing it on purpose, you weren't doing it to hurt her. Any more than your father was doing it to hurt you."

I said that we had had dinner with Quintana over the weekend, and talked to her on the phone since. She had expressed at dinner the feeling that she did not yet "feel as great" as she had thought she would after quitting, that it had "not sunk in yet." I had let this go at the time – I didn't want to seize on it and make her feel we were ganging up on her in some way – but when I talked to her on the phone and a similar feeling was expressed I had suggested that maybe she was still feeling too traumatized by everything that had happened to address the question of what happens next. And that the sense of exhilaration or freedom wouldn't really come until she had sorted all that out, gotten started down a new road.

"Good. That was valuable, that's going to stick with her. Because you expressed it in an empathetic way. Rather than in a way she could interpret as accusing."

I said she and I were going to the Blessing of the Animals at St. John the Divine on Sunday and I was going to try to talk to her more about this.

"Just keep it on that empathetic level. Don't make the mistake of telling her what to do, telling her what she should be doing. You can't teach by telling. Trying to teach by telling is very hard not to do. It seems counterintuitive. It seems to run against human nature. Which is to say it runs against the way we ourselves were taught. This is one of the hardest things to learn when you're being trained as a psychiatrist. Again and again, when I was in training and having to present my case studies, I'd see the mistakes I'd made in the interview. I'd tried to tell. And the patient had closed off."

I said that I had also been thinking about reasons why Quintana had not developed or had lost self-esteem. There were points in which her school experience had probably worked to make her feel less than adequate. I told him about the reading/meaning difficulty, which had set her back when she began Westlake. And then she had seemed to get it, get it all, and by the time she was a senior she had seemed on top of the world. I told him about the conversation I had this morning with Dorothy LoCastro, and Dorothy saying she didn't see any way to sell a thirteen-year-old girl self-esteem.

"There isn't," he said. "Or a thirteen-year-old boy. It's misery. But it does get better. As you say it did for Quintana. Always at about that age."

Then, I said, they go to college, and they plummet again. I said that I had become convinced that unless a child is deeply committed to some discipline, college is a terrible, terrible idea.

"I couldn't agree with you less. College is, or should be, about discovering the world. That's what it always was, particularly when there's a strong core curriculum. You discover things you never knew. I didn't have that experience. It was wartime, and I joined the Navy and went to college and medical school at the same time. All in two years. It was a fast-track program to produce doctors for the Navy. I was at Princeton, but it was nothing like a Princeton experience. We ate Navy rations on Navy metal trays. I never took a history course or an English course or any course at all that wasn't applied to medical training. I miss that now. Especially when I travel. I find I know nothing."

I said that Quintana did not go to a college with a strong, or even any, core curriculum. She went for two years to Bennington, then transferred to Barnard, but by then a certain amount of damage had been done.

"The most unstructured environment possible. She was the classic wrong candidate for Bennington or Sarah Lawrence, from everything I know about her."

I said that part of it was my fault. I had wanted myself to go to Bennington but my father wouldn't let me. So I had encouraged her to go to a summer program there in high school, which she had loved, everybody wore leotards and smoked cigarettes and read Sartre, what high school girl wouldn't love it. Then, when the time came to apply for colleges, her guidance counselor kept steering her there. She had low SATs. The guidance counselor kept telling her she couldn't get in anywhere else. Which even at the time we didn't think was true – she had other things going for her – but she took the path of least resistance and applied for early admission.

"She could have gotten into most colleges in this country. Of course she had other things going for her. But she couldn't believe that about herself."

I said we literally took her out after two years. Told her to go to Europe. In the course of researching Europe she discovered Barnard, and "had to go there". So that was great, and made us feel really mad – partly at ourselves – about the Bennington experience.

4 October 2000

I said that Q and I had gone to the Blessing of the Animals on
Sunday. That it had been very beautiful, theatrical, exhausting,
and in some way very troubling, upsetting, something I couldn't
quite get out of my mind. At one point during the service I
had become afraid that the ribbons would catch fire from the
candles, that a fire would break out and we would be trapped.
There was a pagan aspect. The music. The crowds. The animals
in the cathedral. Quintana's reaction, which had surprised me.
She had seemed uneasy with certain aspects of the situation –
the emotional response to the mass, the joining of hands,
the openness of expression. This uneasiness or shyness was
something I hadn't expected in this particular situation. I said
one reading in particular had struck me. It was a part of the
Gospel I had always disliked intensely – the part about "consider
the lilies of the field, they toil not, neither do they spin" – which
had always seemed to me to undermine everything that made the
world as I understood it work. But this time – maybe because it
was a new translation – I noticed the two lines at the end. "Do
not worry about tomorrow, for tomorrow will bring worries of its
own. Today's trouble is enough for today."

And, I said, I realized that this is what I had been doing.
Worrying about tomorrow. Anticipating the worst possible
outcome.

"Exactly," he said. "Since earliest childhood. Worrying is all
mixed up in your mind with loving. You don't think you can love
without worrying."

I said I wish I could believe, vis-à-vis Quintana, that my worries
were groundless.

"You don't have to think they're groundless. You have to ask
yourself what purpose they serve. They can't help Quintana, so
are they helping you? On the evidence, all your worries are doing
is tying both of you in knots. You can't do for her what she has

to do for herself. There's such a thing in the world as prudent preventive maintenance. You do it on your house, you do it with your health. People who don't do this end up with much bigger problems. There's a kind of personality, however, for whom preventive maintenance takes over. They're always painting the house. They're always worrying about something they've supposedly left undone. That's where you are. Did your parents worry about you?"

I said I supposed they had, I didn't know.

"When that pattern is present, it persists into adult life."

I said that in fact my parents had seemed constantly worried about me as an adult, so maybe they had been the same way when I was a child. I mentioned their aversion to my driving, and Daddy sleeping in the living room when I was in Sacramento. That to one side, I said, I realized that it was imperative for me to get beyond this pattern of worrying, of obsessing on some possible downside. I said that it had in fact led to a fight this week between you and me of a type and intensity that we hadn't experienced since the early years of our marriage.

"How did it start?"

I said it started over my worrying out loud at dinner over how our November trip to Paris would go. Whether Quintana would really want to go, or be able to go. Et cetera.

"Anticipating the worst?"

Yes, I said.

"And then where did it go?"

Downhill, I said.

"He thought you weren't taking into account what he thought or wanted or was worried about?"

That would sum it up, I said.

"You weren't. He's as worried as you are, but he recognizes that the two of you have a life to live. Did you ever think of saying 'Never mind what Quintana wants, you and I need to get away, let's go to Paris by ourselves'?"

That's what I was thinking, I said, but I didn't say it, no.

"It's pretty obvious everybody in your family would be a lot better off if everybody – you and Quintana in particular – actually said what you were thinking. If you get any hint from Quintana that she's resistant to this trip, I think you should say, flat out, 'you do what you want, your father and I will do what we want.' She can take this. She's a lot better, you know. A lot stronger. According to Dr. Kass, she's in no way as weak as she was."

I said I thought we were both at this juncture extremely frustrated by not knowing what steps she plans to take next, and frustrated further by trying not to ask her, not to make the plan for her.

"Do not make the plan for her."

I said we knew that, but it was hard. For example I had picked up a magazine I thought would be a possible market for her. I had mentioned it to her in the most casual way possible – mentioned too that the editor was an acquaintance of ours, knew her, and was AA. And she had said right, she knew the magazine, in fact she had shot for it. What she did not say – or even acknowledge when I mentioned it – was that it might be a good idea to make contact with this magazine.

"Leave that to Dr. Kass. Dr. Kass is very, very good at guiding her into that kind of connection. That kind of plan, if you will."

11 October 2000

I sat down and immediately began to cry.

"What's on your mind," Dr. MacKinnon asked.

I said I didn't know. I rarely cried. In fact I never cried in crises. I just found it very difficult to sit down facing somebody and talk.

"Of course you don't cry in the course of your day, whoever was around would feel you were accusing them of hurting you in some way. They would feel guilty. This isn't the course of your day. I don't feel guilty. You find it difficult to talk today in particular?"

I said no, every day.

"But you mention it today."

I said that I mentioned it today because it seemed to me particularly striking that I sat down and immediately reacted (to nothing but his silence) by crying. In light of the fact that I actually felt quite good – felt maybe as if I might be capable of seeing daylight for the first time in a long while – I could only conclude that I was finding it almost impossible to be forced to express myself.

"Who's forcing you," he said.

That's why I'm here, I said. I can't just sit here in silence.

"You could if you wanted to," he said. "But I think you'd be better off thinking about what these tears are expressing. Tears express a lot of things, particularly in people whose wiring is as close to the surface as yours is. They can express relief, joy, all kinds of complicated emotions in between. You said you were feeling that you might be capable of seeing daylight."

I said I had experienced – just yesterday – a kind of breakthrough about what I could do next. I had finished the long political piece I'd been doing. It was over, I'd seen it in print over the weekend.

Then the question of what to do next – a decision I'd been putting off, not addressing – had become urgent. At some point yesterday it had occurred to me that I could take a couple of long pieces I'd done about California and use them – one of them in particular – as notes for an extended essay or book about California. These pieces dealt with things that had been very much on my mind all this year – really for years before that, but this year in particular because the attitudes implicit in them had been things we talked about all year. For example the basic story of the crossing – the redemption through survival, the redemption for what purpose, the nihilism. The fables and the confusion they engendered.

"I can see that as thrilling," he said. "Liberating. I could make a case that you walked in here and sat down and for the first time felt liberated enough to cry, tears of joy. You'd found something you thought could truly engage you, enable you to set your concerns to one side. Which is what you've needed to do all year. It was the clearest thing about you. You needed to work, and work in a meaningful way. It's not selfish. It's crucial to your own survival."

I said we had for all intents and purposes shelved the movie business. We had been tending in that direction all year, but finally the impulse had gone critical.

"One of the first things I remember your telling me was about a meeting in California that had upset you, depressed you. Obviously, for whatever reason – some of which surely had to do with the youth orientation of the industry – this wasn't improving your situation."

Only monetarily, I said. And that would be something we'd have to figure out, deal with.

"You're very strong. You'll be amazed what you can deal with if you're doing something you want to be doing."

I said we had seen Quintana Friday night, her last day at work. She had been late to dinner and come into the restaurant in some distress. It had seemed to both of us that she might have had a few drinks but we really didn't know. In any case, we had heard nothing about what she plans to do. What she had told us instead was that she was seeing someone she liked a lot, someone she had met at an AA meeting. The AA meeting had been the encouraging part. He was 48. He had three children by two marriages. This did not per se concern me. What did concern me in a nagging way was that this sudden attachment to an older man very much echoed an attachment she had formed at the very moment when she had previously quit a job to undertake a freelance life. There was a fear that the energy she needed to undertake this life would go into the attachment, that the attachment had in the first case and could in this case serve as a kind of way out.

"That seems quite possible, but I would hope very strongly that you never communicate this concern to her."

I said I hadn't, and wouldn't, but it was a concern. On the other hand I could hardly begrudge her a boyfriend. I would just like to know what she's going to do.

"I doubt very much if she knows what she's going to do."

Don't you think we should talk to her about it, I said. Help her formulate a plan.

"No. Absolutely not. And if that moment comes when she asks you what you think she should do, don't fall into the trap. Don't let her set you up. Just say that she'll know what to do, and when she has some specific idea that she wants your advice on, you'll be glad to help."

But what if she needs help, I said.

"Let her ask Dr. Kass. She and Dr. Kass talk in this area constantly. Take yourself off the hook here. Because anything specific you suggest will be read as trying to box her into a program not her own."

I said that we and Dr. Kass had in fact seen that dynamic vis-à-vis rehab. The idea that she was drinking too much had been entirely her own. She had asked a friend for help. The friend had suggested rehab. She had herself called Hazelden. Once the idea of rehab had graduated into a given, she was quite firm about Hazelden. It wasn't our idea. Minnesota wasn't even on our map. Say rehab to me, I think Betty Ford. I had in fact talked to Betty Ford, offered her that option. No, she had said. Hazelden. There's a Hazelden in West Palm Beach, we had said. No, she had said. Hazelden Minnesota. Then, later, after she was home and had a relapse and we saw Dr. Kass, he had mentioned that he had been a little troubled by her tendency to speak of the decision to go to Hazelden as someone else's, a fait accompli thrust upon her. I had noticed this too.

"That's the dynamic I'm talking about. Don't let her do it. Sooner or later, she'll realize that she has to order her days, make Tuesday different from Sunday, say. There are too many reality cues for her not to get it. Very soon, she's going to notice that everybody she talks to asks her what do you do, what are you doing. She's going to have to come up with an adequate answer. She won't need you to tell her that. In fact you can't tell her that. Only her peers can tell her. Meanwhile, you and John concentrate on your own work."

18 October 2000

I said that all my concerns about Q – when we spoke last week –
had turned out to be groundless. That during the past week
she had seemed in many ways a different person – that she had
interviewed for and gotten a six-week freelance picture editing
job at a Conde Nast magazine, that her hostility toward working
seemed to have evaporated, that she had broken up with the new
boyfriend I had feared was a way out of facing what she had to
do – far from wanting a way out, she had broken up with him
precisely because she felt he was keeping her from doing what she
needed to do.

"In other words a markedly more mature attitude," he said.

Exactly, I said. She had even been assertive enough to establish
in her initial interview that she would be going to Paris
Thanksgiving week. She seemed to be in a place that was the
very opposite of where I'd assumed she was.

"Still, I wouldn't say your fears were groundless," he said.
"You had grounds for them, all right. The grounds were in your
head."

I said in other words absurd, of no importance.

"No," he said. "It is important, and it's not absurd. What's in
your head – what you think or assume or anticipate about her –
has everything to do with how the two of you deal with each
other. That's why you and I sit here every week. So you can find
out what's in your head." A change of subject: "Right now, you
must be feeling considerable relief."

I said that both you and I were very relieved. That you had said
it was the first time in over a year that you hadn't had a knot in
your stomach. That we were aware that there would be downs,
but this was the strongest up we had experienced.

"Naturally there'll be downs. Life has downs."

I said we were just beginning to refocus on our own work. That you had done a very fast piece on deadline for the New Yorker, were closing it this week, and next week would go back to your novel. I was starting the book I had mentioned about California. There was another thing. This morning you had mentioned rereading part of a novel you had published several books back, and being amazed at how much you had known. I have myself had this sense reading old things of mine. I had said this morning that I thought a lot of this knowledge we now felt we didn't have had come from reporting, getting out into the world in a way we hadn't been doing. And it had occurred to me at some point during the day that this past year and a half had worked to confirm the idea that we shouldn't be out extending ourselves in the world – that we had felt in a real way on constant call, emergency duty at home.

"By getting out into the world do you mean traveling?"

Not exclusively, I said, but that's part of it. A great amount of work that both of us did had come indirectly from trips we had taken to South Asia and to Central and South America and to the Middle East. You don't necessarily go to write something, but you end up using it.

"If you're going to do that, now's the time to do it. Later on you lack the energy."

I said we lacked the energy now, but I thought it was important we start thinking in terms of expending the energy we still have. That if the opportunity arose to do something that interested one or another of us, we should just do it.

"You seem to see it as an exercise. A way of sharpening your skills, your ability to analyze."

I said yes. The ability to analyze and the ability to notice. We had for example once spent an entirely arduous day visiting a Palestinian refugee camp outside Amman. Nothing came of this, but that one experience had enabled me to know from the outset that Arafat would be unable to control the generation of Palestinians growing up in the camps.

A brief discussion of the Middle East, the Cole, and the danger to traveling Americans. This segued into a discussion of my mother, and her "I just don't understand anything". Her saying this about Steven's divorce, and also saying "maybe they just had too much, maybe if I hadn't given them that money every year . . ."

"Oh, no," Dr. MacKinnon said. "You certainly come naturally by that excessive reflex for assuming your own guilt. Take a lesson from that. And tell her any money she gave them probably kept them together a year longer than they might have lasted without it."

I asked if he had read the piece in this morning's paper about a new theory of not praising children.

"I certainly did," he said. "What did you think of it?"

I said that I myself had never witnessed these examples of parents praising children for nothing.

"Not the way you and I were brought up, certainly. I thought it was largely wrongheaded, but I did see a few points. For example the instance they brought up of responding to a child who gives an older person his seat by saying 'notice how much the lady appreciated your giving her your seat,' instead of praising the child for doing the right thing. There's a point there. It teaches the child to actually empathize with the woman instead of just 'doing the right thing'."

Maybe so, I said, but what if the woman *doesn't* appreciate the gesture?

"I see your point. You could be making the child dependent on the positive feedback he or she might not get. Whereas the feedback for 'doing the right thing' comes from within, the child can award it to him or herself."

I said the only part that had interested me had to do with 'working mothers' having this tendency to overpraise, not wanting to spoil their limited time with the child. It seemed to me that I had possibly occasionally refrained from negative responses to something Quintana did, just because I didn't want to spoil the moment. This brought up the whole question of 'working mothers'. It had occurred to me today – probably because I've been reading these emigrant accounts, in which mothers definitely worked and often neglected their 7 or 8 or even 12 children – that there must have been only a very brief period in the history of America when women *didn't* work. *Didn't* help run the farm or feed 20 farm hands three meals a day and do all the washing by hand. You would think this notion of women not working only came along with labor-saving appliances – after WW2 – but it was already ingrained in my grandmother and mother. Who came from families in which women had in fact worked hard.

"Absolutely," he said. "It was a class thing that developed. If you were off the farm, women shouldn't have to work. Even at the bottom of the depression, middle class women didn't work. In Leonia, New Jersey, where I grew up, every single woman I knew had a maid. That freed them to play bridge or roll bandages or whatever they did. But they didn't work. A lot of this lingers on. As recently as 1975, when our daughter moved to Seattle and passed the bar examination, the man who admitted her to the bar told her that he hoped she was satisfied, she was coming from an eastern law school to take the place of a well-trained local man so she could hold a job she'd give up as soon as she had a baby. You don't think any of this got into your head, but it had to."

1 November 2000

Brief discussion the USS Cole and his Seattle trip.

I told him about our two conversations (if they could be so called)
with Quintana this afternoon. I said I – we both – were so tired
of being up and down on this. Of charting every encounter. I said
that when I last spoke to him – two weeks ago – she had seemed
so in charge that I had been euphoric with relief. Then she started
work on this short-term assignment, and seemed plunged into
fear she couldn't handle it. We had assured her that was the way
everybody felt in a new job – that every day would get better.
And for a few days it had. At some point last week we had had
these very good telephone calls – about "The Night of the Living
Dead", which she and I had seen when she was a child – followed
up by some very good emails – and I had thought everything was
fine. Over the weekend we heard nothing. You had had a dream
about her, which you told me about because you had dreamed
it in color and she and we had discussed – vis a vis the sequel to
"Night of the Living Dead" – whether people dream in color or
only in black and white.

"Some people do dream in color," he interrupted.

I said that in fact Q had said that. She had read that "more
creative" people dream in color.

"That seems to be true. People with strong visual sense.
Musicians on the other hand have aural dreams. I myself
began dreaming in color for the first time during the course
of my analysis. People who dream in color describe the color
as unrealistic, like old-fashioned Technicolor, almost surreal.
There's usually a euphoric element in the content of color
dreams."

I said your dream had no euphoric content. It was this: we had
some people at the house and the phone rang and when you
answered it, it was Q. "I'm wrecked," she said. I had asked you

where the color came into it. You said you could see her on a screen or monitor as you talked to her.

In any case, the content of this dream had concerned me – in that it expressed your concern about her, it sort of let my own concern – which had been pushed down – resurface.

So, by today, when we hadn't heard from her, we were both ready to make a call. You had made it, and found her so distressed that I called and asked her to dinner. I said I didn't understand what it was in this work situation that was making her so upset. It was basically the same job she'd been doing successfully for six years.

"I think I'd wonder if possibly it's not her work situation that's upsetting her."

You mean something else could be upsetting her, and she transfers it onto work? I asked.

"Isn't that usually the case?"

I allowed that it was.

"Couldn't she be upset – at a deeper level than she knows – by what you described as the very good conversations you had about 'The Night of the Living Dead'? You said you and she had watched it together when she was a child. Tell me a little more about that. How old was she?"

I said about seven. You had been out of town. She and I had watched it in your office in Malibu, which was all French doors onto the sea. And it had been so scary that about midnight – when I had to go into the kitchen – I'd been afraid to leave her alone in the office, I made her come with me. I told her I was too scared to go into the kitchen alone.

"Let's take this step by step. In the first place, what were you doing letting a seven-year-old watch so scary a movie at midnight?"

That's why I was watching it with her, I said.

"Didn't you have curfews? Did she usually stay up until midnight? Could she watch any scary thing she wanted on television?"

I said she only watched two or three things on television. She watched reruns of Julia Child, she watched reruns of Lucy, and she watched "Creature Features", which was horror movies.

"And you didn't think they would scare her?"

I said they scared me more than they scared her.

"Well, there we are. That's my point. Is there anything you'd do differently if you could replay this particular night?"

I asked what it was he thought I should have done differently, other than put her to bed, which didn't seem like being a fun mom.

"You told her you were afraid to go into the kitchen alone, so you wanted her to go with you. What do you think that said to her? Didn't it say she had to be responsible for taking care of you, for protecting you?"

I explained again: I was not actually afraid to go into the kitchen alone, I was afraid to leave her alone by the glass doors.

"Because something might come in and get her. You were afraid in other words you couldn't protect her. This is the very heart of your relationship with her. It doesn't matter which way you put this – you were afraid to go into the kitchen alone or you were afraid to leave her by the glass doors alone – it says the same thing. It says you were afraid you couldn't protect her. It says 'it's an irrational dangerous world out there and I can't protect you from it'. It says she has to protect not only herself but also you. You don't think that's a heavy burden on a seven-year-old?"

I said I could see that it might have been, but I could also see that it was just a movie. I told him about taking her to see "Jaws", through which she screamed with fear and after which she blithely went swimming. I said "Nicholas and Alexandra" was more upsetting to her. She worried about Nicky and Sunny and the children all the way home.

"I'm sure I don't have to spell that one out."

I said I saw his point: Nicky and Sunny were parents unable to protect their children.

"This pattern between you has profoundly to do with your feeling now that you can't protect her. Not this one incident, but what the incident tells us about the relationship you then had with her. She still thinks she has to protect you. And what do you think she has to protect you from? She has to protect you from herself. She knows she could effectively kill both you and her father by hurting herself. That's what she has on you, that's what nobody talks about. This is an extremely delicate negotiation. You want to free her from the guilt, from the responsibility, but at the same time you don't want to let her off that particular hook until she's ready. I think it could be extremely useful if you talked to her about some of what we're talking about today. You don't say 'mea culpa, I did the wrong thing the night we watched The Night of the Living Dead', because somebody as burdened with responsibility as she is tends immediately to say no, no, you're not guilty, I'm guilty. What we have to get rid of here is the idea that anybody has to be guilty. Things happen, sometimes bad things. Nobody has to be blamed. Melanie Klein was the one who did the brilliant work on this. Most religions get into this area of absolving people of blame. Yours and mine doesn't happen to do the best job of it, but the thought is still buried there, right in 'Forgive us our trespasses, as we forgive . . .' So. When you talk about this, don't assume guilt, and don't let her assume it. Talk about how essentially strong she must have been, and how strong you actually are to be able to admit your mistakes. Be careful, but do talk about it, because it's very close to the heart of the problem here."

We then talked about my California book,* about Jane Hollister Wheelwright, and her idealized and very confused view of her own life. Despite the fact that she was an analyst. I said it had been very stunning to me on this rereading of her book that she was unable to sort out the truth and untruth in her view of her own life – if she couldn't do it, a trained analyst, it made me wonder if I could ever do it myself.

"That's why this is a very good time for you to be doing this particular book. It bears directly on what we're talking about here. I think this book – more than anything else you could be doing right now – can take you into areas that are going to help you integrate your life. You've done a lot of moving on. It's time you picked up some of the pieces you left behind and figured out what they meant to you."

I said that this had been my somewhat inchoate thought, but it was already taking me into areas where I wasn't sure I wanted to go.

"Absolutely it will. Count on it. And if you get into one of those areas, and you don't immediately have an appointment with me, give me a call."

* *Where I Was From.*

8 November 2000

Some chat about election, which Dr. MacKinnon believes will end in court, "because you don't bring in Warren Christopher unless you mean to go to court."

I said that when I saw him last Wednesday we had been expecting to have dinner with Quintana that night, but that she had canceled. We had been unable to see her over the weekend, she had a friend in town. I explained Nicola's history, and Quintana's having to follow up her last visit with a week in detox. I explained about your calling her at work on Monday and finding her at home. I explained our distress. I described my call to her, and her saying "please don't worry, I can get through this," and my saying "all right, if you tell me not to worry, I won't."

"I'm struck by the similarity of this story to the story you told me last week. In both instances, you're fearful, you're worried, and in both instances you let her know that only she can relieve this fear, only she can be responsible for your peace of mind."

I said that I myself was under no illusions that I handled this right.

"I discussed that story – the one about the movie – with Dr. Kass. He too found it very to the point. Very useful to him. Both you and John tend to be worriers. This tendency to worry in both cases predated the arrival of Quintana. But once she was there – all of your worries and fears focused on her safety. You wanted to keep her in the kitchen with you, safe from the terrifying world outside. Where people might kidnap her, might hurt her, might take her away from you. Which would effectively end your life. That's what you transmitted to her, that's the burden she feels. That's why she feels that you and her father are always watching her, always trying to take care of her. She knows it's because you love her, she got that message. But she associates love with worry. She doesn't know that it's possible to love someone without constantly worrying about him or her. She thinks she has to worry about you, because she loves you. She thinks she's a burden on you. She thinks that only she can relieve that burden. You see this very clearly with suicidal patients. First they see themselves as a burden, then they think that it's up to them to remove that burden, then at some point they decide you'll be better off without them. This moment of decision is always two-edged. One, they'll themselves be once and for all escaping your constant worry. Two, by freeing themselves they'll free you."

I suggested that if she did in fact associate love with worry it would be very hard – and counterproductive – to tell her I didn't worry about her.

"Yes. It's delicate. These things are so mixed up by the time somebody reaches her age that it's very hard to know which thread you can pull. Incidentally, I should tell you that Dr. Kass is not at the present time worried about the possibility of suicide with Quintana. She seems to have some life outside the two of you. She has other relationships. As long as she maintains this other life, she's not a suicide risk."

I showed him the e-mail she had sent yesterday.

"Look at what she says," he said. " 'I'm so sorry to have this affliction.' 'Worry you both so much.' 'Such a burden'. 'So sorry to put you through this'. That's what we've been talking about. Something positive here, however, is the apparent freedom with which she can say 'I love you'. Which means that you and John clearly feel the same freedom saying it to her, because otherwise she wouldn't have learned how. Or she would have learned not to."

I said that as a family we had never had any trouble expressing love. Which seemed in some way miraculous to me, because the expression of love was so freighted in my own family as to approach paralysis.

"You know, I've come to understand why Dr. Kass wanted you to see me. It didn't have to do just with Quintana's concern about your being depressed, although that was a factor. It turns out that what we're doing here is trying to break the pattern in which you focus all of your worries and fears on Quintana. Not that this is one-way. Not by any means. She searches out your worries and fears, she feeds on them. They make her feel loved and they make her feel that she has a purpose in life: she's here to give you peace of mind."

I asked if he truly thought that was how she saw her purpose in life.

"Unfortunately, when you don't have a strong self-image, the imagined need to take care of someone else can fill the void. But the person who fills the void that way ultimately resents it. You've become much more able to talk to Quintana about your own relationship with her. This has been extremely valuable. She talks about what you've said to Dr. Kass, and it opens up areas he wouldn't have been able to reach on his own. He thinks she's not an easy person to reach. You're a big help in this."

I said that he had urged me last week to talk to her about some of this, of "The Night of the Living Dead". I hadn't, because I hadn't seen her. Did he think it would be a good idea for me to talk to her tonight about some of what we'd talked about today?

"Absolutely I do. If you just try to give her a sense that she can gain strength by talking about things, you'll be on safe ground. And any time you find an opportunity to let her know she doesn't have to be like you, that she can create a world of her own, do it."

I said I sometimes thought the way she dressed was an expression of not being like me. She didn't dress the way I did. She wouldn't buy things that I would buy.

"Good," he said. "Don't discourage it."

You mentioned her having a weak self-image, I said. I said I thought her being overweight was an expression of this. Of course she put on a lot of weight when she was drinking too much, but she had always had a tendency, and I thought it was a problem with her – it took her, at some dim level, out of competition.

"When did she start gaining weight?"

Early adolescence, I said. Then as she got more confident in late adolescence she lost it, but it came back when she went to college and lost confidence.

"You don't think in early adolescence she was sending you a message?" he asked.

A message she was unhappy? I asked.

"No. A message she could do something you could never do. You couldn't gain weight if you wanted to. And you may well have wanted to. You were the one who could do everything, but only she could do this."

29 November 2000

Discussion of how I felt and was dealing with this. "There's nothing about a broken hip that's per se depressing," Dr. MacKinnon said, "but things like this do tend to have a depressing effect."

I said yes, there was something about a broken hip that was per se depressing. Broken hip reads "old". Broken leg, broken arm reads . . .

"Somehow different," he agreed. "Especially for women."

I said we had been struck by how alarming the idea of a broken hip was to many women we knew. It seemed to tap into a quite widespread fear. Something like "bag lady".

"Same fear," he said. "Fear of being old, being dependent, being unable to take care of yourself, being cast aside."

I said we had had a very nice quiet Thanksgiving – the Indian lunch, the caviar with Q – but had decided not to do Christmas Eve. In a lot of ways this was a relief, yet at some level I felt guilty about it – I know I'll be feeling much more up to things by Christmas, and in that light not doing the party could be an instance of isolating ourselves.

"People's patterns of entertaining change as they get older. Great friends of ours used to have a party every New Year's day. A tradition, we always went. Then it was every other year. I just happened to realize, it's been three years now, and if they're doing it this year we haven't been invited. Entertaining takes a certain amount of energy. Not just physical energy, emotional energy. You tend to conserve that energy as you age. You want it there for what really matters to you. As far as isolating yourself goes, that's another pattern of aging. You want to be alone more. You want to be with the people you care most about. All these casual friendships are very exciting when you're young – you don't know where they might lead, they're mysteries. They're not so much mysteries any more. You've been there."

I said that my parents used to always have parties on New Year's Day and on the Fourth of July. And that when they stopped I thought it was sad, that they should make more effort. Maybe in retrospect they didn't want to make the effort. I don't think they ever had another party after Mother had cancer in 1984. That year was very hard not only on her but on my father. He couldn't seem to get it through his head that the treatment was helping her. He kept telling me the doctors were poisoning her, she'd be perfectly fine without this goddamn medicine they were giving her. I felt at the time that he was blaming me to some extent, because I was the one who pressed her to do chemotherapy.

"Having cancer changes your life radically," Dr. MacKinnon said. "Even if you survive the ten years, which is like saying you're 'cured', you've still had ten years of wondering when it's going to kick back in. Of facing mortality. Or not facing it. Whatever your strategy, it has to change your life."

I said I thought it was five years.

"That's what they used to say. Recently they're upping it."

I said that my strategy for dealing with cancer didn't include facing mortality. I had real trouble thinking of myself as dead.

"Everybody does. You can think of dying, because in some ways it's active, it's happening to you, you're an actor in it. But it's impossible to truly conceive of not being."

I said I had been thinking about this since I was a very small child. Not of "dying", but of "being" and "not being". I can remember trying to turn around very fast to see if the world in fact existed if I didn't see it.

"I can see another possible interpretation on that. You were trying to find out what was going on behind your back. Children in families where emotion doesn't get expressed – in other words children who grew up in families like you or I did – are always trying to find out what's going on. They're intensely curious about their parents. Their parents are extremely mysterious to them, and often glamourous."

I said that all adults – adult life in general – had been glamourous to me as a child, but that this had changed between my and Quintana's generation. Adults hadn't seemed to interest her much – she was good with them but didn't see them as mysteries. It was her peers that seemed to mystify her.

"I don't see your household as one in which much was hidden or left unexpressed. I think you and John were much more out front with her than her grandparents' generation would have been."

I said that Q and I were having dinner tomorrow night. You and I were to have gone to a party where there would be a lot of people and stairs, I had told you to go and asked Q to dinner. She had immediately translated this into her cooking dinner for me, which was another instance I supposed of her feeling guilty about me, having to take care of me.

"Why do you assume she feels guilty?"

Because she said the week after this happened that she felt guilty, she "should be up here every night cooking for you."

"She wasn't, was she?"

No, I said.

"So she can't have felt too guilty."

I said I thought she set herself up to feel guilty. To think she "should" be doing something, then to not do it, then to feel guilty.

"That's possible, but there's another possibility. That she wants to express her love for you. And that you respond – because you don't want to be a burden – by telling her in effect that you don't need her help, you can take care of yourself, you're perfectly fine. I think this confusion between love and guilt begins in your mind. I think you got it from your parents, who never wanted to be a burden on you. You didn't tell me that, but I think it's true, because not being a burden on any other member of the family was a very big issue among parents who came of age in the depression. I think it's important that you try to sort this out – acknowledge the possibility of love without guilt – because it could be very valuable to her to be able to do something freely for you. To cook you dinner if she will. Doing for the people we love can be a source of tremendous pleasure. Satisfaction. Pride. Don't deny her that."

6 December 2000

I said it had been a really terrible week.

He said that he had spoken to Dr. Kass. "I straightened out that misunderstanding you mentioned, and in the course of the conversation he indicated that Quintana was not entirely past her alcoholism."

I told him what had happened, beginning with her and my dinner Thursday night. The discussion of the day-treatment program. My reading or misreading of her anxiety and depression as a "real life" problem, part and parcel of any creative or free-lance endeavor, something you had to learn to bull your way through or work your way around, learn tricks to handle it.

"Absolutely it is," he said.

And, I said, because I wasn't figuring alcohol into it as the problem it seemed to be, I had encouraged her to take this other short-term job and then see how she felt – the program would still be there four weeks from now, and by then – with the positive feedback and reinforcement of feeling needed and useful at work – she might have discovered a fresh approach to beginning her own work. She had seemed to agree with this, had said she felt much better having talked it through, and had left. In the morning she had called to say that she had talked to Dr. Kass, had turned down the job, but had still not decided what to do about the program. We had said in essence that this was a no-brainer, if she had turned down the job she might as well do the program.

Then her arrival Friday afternoon. She had been drinking. She had been walked up from her apartment by this man she was suddenly seeing again who had been a kind of negative influence or way out the last time she tried to work free lance. He had apparently told her she needed to detox, he couldn't watch her this way.

She said that she had been drinking since around the time she left Elle Décor, but it was impossible to know. She doesn't tell the truth about drinking, or maybe she doesn't know the truth. For example when you asked her the longest she had been sober she said "90 days", and I had said did that include Hazelden and she had said no, it was the 90 days after Hazelden. But it wasn't. Because she got out of Hazelden August 4 1999 and on the morning of August 31 we got the call in Paris.

"She can't face knowing the truth. Dr. Kass wants her to do Twelve-Step, you know."

I said I knew that. That he had explained that the purpose of the day-treatment program was to enable or prepare her to do Twelve-Step. That she was incapable of doing it because she had personality disorders that prevented her from doing it.

"That's what he told me. I agree with him."

I told him about her reaction to the Sunday meeting at St. James.

"You saw an example of what Dr. Kass meant, then."

I said that in a lot of ways she still reacted to people the way an adolescent would.

"There's a lot of adolescent still in her. Plus some pre-adolescent. I think the program will help her, but it's going to mean she'll be a drag on you for a period of time."

I said we recognized that.

"Just don't let yourself get involved in it. If she wants to talk about it, fine, but don't ask her about it, don't become her arbiter. She'll try to make you that. Just keep out of it, be neutral, say 'that would be an interesting thing to discuss in the group.' In other words make her assert herself, deal with the situation herself."

I said that this episode had been very hard on both of us.

"Why particularly this time? You've been through this before, you'll probably go through it again."

I said that was exactly why it was hard on us. We didn't see any longterm hope. And there were things that she said that were very upsetting to us. For example when she turned on me for "always talking about work, all you care about is work," etc.

"That's typical alcoholic behavior. It's always someone else's fault."

I said that there was something about this weekend that was so extremely upsetting to me that I could hardly mention it: it had occurred to me at several points that I didn't *like* her.

"Of course it did. This is very aggravating to deal with, you lose patience. It's aggravating to Dr. Kass. I had to point out to him that he had a personally aggrieved tone when he talked about her. 'She's really a hard-core alcoholic,' he said to me, as if this had just occurred to him. 'What did you think she was,' I asked him."

I said it was one thing for Dr. Kass to feel personally aggrieved, it was another for me, because I was her mother. And there was another thing. All my life I have turned away from people who were trouble to me. Cut them out of my life. I can't have that happen with Quintana.

"It won't. It can't possibly. You have too strong a maternal instinct. Even today, when I saw you in the waiting room, you were looking at pictures in National Geographic of polar bears and their cubs. You put it down to come in here with real regret. But let's talk for a minute about the reason you cut people off. You cut them off ultimately to protect yourself, but first of all to protect them from your anger. You're afraid of your own anger. You think it's so powerful that it would destroy these people you're mad at, and then you wouldn't have the relationship any more."

I don't have it anyway, I pointed out, since I cut them off.

"They don't always know they're cut off, do they?"

Not always, I said.

"So in theory you could forgive them, resume the relationship."

I said I didn't see where this was going. I said this had just been a very hard time. You and I really liked to control things. And this past month had been a period when we were totally unable to control anything – reaching a grand crescendo Friday afternoon.

"What makes this situation with Quintana so particularly aggravating to you – and part of what makes you feel anger toward her, and guilty about feeling it – could be that deep down you think she could control it if she wanted to. She could decide to commit herself to 12-step, she could decide not to take that drink."

I said yes. This was true. I could not escape the sense that she could control her situation if she wanted to. But it wasn't for me a question of deciding to take or not take that drink. What I thought she could control was the way she handled taking that drink. So she slipped. So what would be lost if she forced herself to get up in the morning and go to work?

"That's a strategy – setting everything else aside and going to work – that's worked very well for you. It's still the best way to allay anxiety known to man. Work. Better than drugs, better even than alcohol. But she doesn't have the faith in her work that you have in yours. When she does, she'll be for all intents and purposes cured."

I said I hadn't been able to work lately. I said neither had you.

"You have to get back to work. Both of you. It's what makes you function. You have to lead your lives as if this weren't happening, at the same time recognizing that it is. For you to fall apart now would be the worst possible thing that could happen to her."

13 December 2000

Discussion of how I felt, re my hip. I told him I was much
stronger – really almost physically normal – but mentally shaky,
fragile, too easily exhausted. I was exhausted for example by
the party Thursday night, although I'd done nothing. I told him
what had happened Friday night – the reading, the Hedermans,
suddenly knowing I had to go home. I said I had been wondering
if this kind of injury did something to your brain – although I
hadn't hit my head at all.

"Of course it does," he said. "Any injury like that makes you feel
fragile, incapable. It affects your self-image in a negative way.
You have it fixed in your mind that you can't fall. It's the most
important thing on your mind: not falling. You move differently,
you perceive your surroundings differently. I was on crutches for
three months after I fell last winter. I'd never before been nervous
walking around this neighborhood after dark. But on crutches I
was. I felt like prey. Then – even after I was off crutches – I had
to cancel a trip to see my daughter in Seattle. Which made me
feel new limits. I managed to go to a big school reunion, but I
was miserable, I was only thinking about not getting hurt. Then I
realized there was no point going to Europe, which we usually do
every September. It makes you feel old. Useless. Never mind you
didn't hit your head. It still affects your head."

I said I supposed that the strain of last week had intensified this
feeling of fragility. Last night I had even found myself wondering
if – if I were to go see my mother in January – I would be able to
drive.

"You'll remember how to drive, but I understand why you feel
that. I understand that Quintana seems better."

I said yes, she did. When we talked to her on Sunday we had both
been somewhat encouraged – she spoke of "having nine days"
without either false euphoria or the kind of defensiveness we'd
come to see as a danger signal.

We talked about the Supreme Court decision. I said I had found it depressing, troubling in some way that didn't have anything to do with who got to be president.

"What they did or what they didn't do?"

What they didn't do, I supposed. I said I always thought I could read Tony Kennedy,* I didn't always agree with his decisions but I knew where they were coming from, they were coming from Sacramento. This was different. I couldn't read it. There was a very clear thing the court could have done, when it came to them the last time, and they didn't do it.

"They were playing out a political game. And the Florida Supreme Court didn't help them, they were playing out their own political game. Obviously, if you wanted to do something that would be the best thing for the country, and wouldn't guarantee one or another political outcome, you would have said at the outset let's recount the entire state and here are the standards we're going to use. Either court could have done that, in plenty of time to get it done. Neither one did."

I said I guess that's what troubled me about it. What troubled me about Tony's role in it. He was smart, he could have seen that. So why didn't he say it?

"He lives in society. A very small, basic society. Those nine people are his society. He has to get along with them in order to function at all."

I said I guessed I still thought of Tony as a child at the dinner table, very smart, very idealistic in some ways – it wasn't a particularly idealistic household, how could it be, his father was Artie Samish's lawyer, his mother was political to the bone, but they were always straight, and Tony was still straight. So it troubled me to see him making this kind of accommodation.

* Anthony Kennedy was a Supreme Court justice from 1988 to 2018. He was born in Sacramento, California. He and Didion grew up together there and remained in touch until her death.

"Most people do make accommodations. You look at this from a very special point of view. You have an unusual purity of intention. You're extremely intelligent, absolutely logical. You demand that everyone else live up to this standard."

I said I didn't live up to it myself.

"Always being right doesn't necessarily make you feel good about yourself."

I said I supposed he was saying that I wasn't always right.

"I'm saying you can't let yourself not be. You can't let yourself make mistakes, be human. Having to be right is like the Midas touch. You think it would be wonderful if everything you touched turned to gold, then you find you've turned to gold yourself, stopped being human."

I said this discussion was kind of striking, because every fight you and I ever had came down to your thinking I was holding myself up as always right. I said I always had trouble understanding this, because I didn't feel right.

"Of course you don't feel right. You could never be right enough to make you feel good about yourself. There's a certain kind of family that encourages the kind of personality you are. Children in that kind of family think if they're right they'll be loved. Then they get to be adults, and they don't understand why being right doesn't make other people love them. And it doesn't. It isolates them. They can't accept other people's mistakes, because they can't accept their own. What's interesting here is that we're talking about the same thing now that we were talking about when you came in. About feeling fragile, threatened by other people, threatened by a world you can't control. What happened to you when you fell is that you lost control. That's the one thing you're most afraid of losing. You don't understand living without control. Which is another way of saying you don't understand not having to be right."

172

20 December 2000

Discussion of Christmas, feeling sandwiched between Mother's depression and Q's depression, usual anxieties of season more vivid to me this year because I don't have a party to focus on, leaving me with sense that I'm "doing" not enough. In fact I did all the necessary presents except for Quintana, which remained a total blank to me. Most years recently we have given her a camera, or some other piece of equipment associated with "career", but I felt constrained about that solution this year, since she had told me a few weeks ago – admittedly she was drunk – that all I ever talked about was her working.

"Does she have a digital camera yet?"

No, I said, and that would be an obvious good idea, if she brought it up, but if she didn't I wasn't sure it was a good idea to feed into what seemed to be a feeling that we were pushing or directing her into working.

"Surely she thinks of her photography as something other than just 'working'?"

I said at this point I really didn't know. She was clearly afraid of it, pushing it off by calling it "working", but on the other hand maybe she really didn't have the temperament to do it. She had the talent, but maybe not the temperament – when you're doing something like that you keep getting rejected, you really don't get positive feedback until you're quite well established – maybe the rejection was too much for her, maybe she should be doing something else, maybe the whole idea of doing something "creative" was based on our having lived that way, maybe she should be reassessing her options.

"This is clearly something she and Dr. Kass are talking about."

I said I didn't know what they talked about. I myself hadn't talked to her about it. Although I had said – a couple of times recently when she was bitching about "hating New York" – that she didn't have to live in New York, she could live anywhere she wanted, she owned her apartment, she could sell it, she could live anywhere she wanted.

"What did she say?"

I said she said it wasn't the right time to think about that. And of course it's not. But I just wanted to open up the idea that she had options, that she could make decisions, change her life.

"I think her affective relationships are too vital to her to consider a move. But I also think that she and Dr. Kass should be exploring her feelings about what she calls 'work'. I asked you once if she'd ever submitted a photograph in any kind of competition."

I said yes, once, in college, and she had won the competition, which involved having the photograph put on a billboard on a highway in New Jersey.

"That's pretty definite feedback. So it's odd she didn't keep competing. I wonder about this."

I said another thing I wasn't sure about was how to handle giving her money. We had told her we were giving her a gift – we had mentioned $100,000 – something that would give her some backup now that she was getting started on her own. But it had always been posited as a kind of "investment", a sum she could use in effect to advance her career. Clearly now – when she was basically in therapy half of her days and not to my knowledge doing anything about working during the remaining half of her days – she was going to need money, just to maintain herself. But this money wasn't meant as maintenance. I couldn't possibly talk to her about this – I was afraid it would just deteriorate into "Doesn't my health come first?"

"I think it would be a lot easier to talk to her if you didn't have an agenda."

Meaning what, I asked.

"Meaning if you weren't always thinking about whether or not you should give her the money. You don't get anywhere by not giving it to her, because A, you'll be wondering every time you talk to her if she has enough money to pay the rent, and B, she'll pick up on why you're not giving it to her, she'll think you're not giving it to her because you don't think she deserves it. So give it to her, take it out of the equation. Just write the check and give it to her, matter-of-fact, as little conversation about it as possible. Don't tell her what to do with it. Knowing your family dynamic, she'll probably think you expect her to turn it over to some family adviser to invest. So let her know she can do that if she wants to, or she can do whatever else she wants. It's hers. End of conversation."

I said I had thought a great deal about our conversation last week about Tony Kennedy, which of course was really a conversation about me. I realized that the strongest strain in my personality was to resist accommodation, to resist playing the game. I said my father had been this way, to a real fault. I saw now that the Kennedys had grown up inside a whole network in which favors could be asked and returned, accommodations made. But I hadn't. For example the "good" summer job if you were in high school in Sacramento was to work the State Fair. Everybody did it. You got these jobs by a parent making a phone call. My father knew the man to call, but would never call.

"Is it possible – to put this in the best light – he was an idealist? He really didn't know how it worked?"

I said I thought it was more likely that he just couldn't ask for favors. I said he had grown up in a peculiar way. His mother died when he was a child, and he and his little brother were sent to live with his father's maiden sister, a woman so incapable and fearful that in another culture or era she probably would have been hospitalized. She was afraid to go out after sundown, she was afraid to ride in – forget drive – a car. To some extent my father was taken in by his mother's family, which he loved, but his father and aunt left their mark. When he went to Berkeley his father would give him no money at all, it wasn't that he didn't have the money, he just didn't think his son should waste time in college. So Daddy had to earn every penny it cost.

"That's an extreme lesson. It had to show up in the way you were raised."

I said it did and it didn't. He wasn't mean, like his father was – his father died when I was in college and I was still calling him "Mr. Didion" – but he had tricky attitudes about money. The one time my mother expressed real anger with him to me was when we first moved to Walnut Road and Jimmy wanted a swimming pool, and Daddy said sure we could have a pool if Jimmy dug it. So all that summer – really hot Sacramento summer – Jimmy tried to dig a pool, on land where the hardpan started about an inch down. And Mother said to me one day, really angry, "look at him out there digging, and even if by some miracle he manages to dig it, your father will never pay to have a pool put in."

"It would be very unusual if some of this sense – if you want a pool, dig it, if you want money, earn it – didn't color this question of giving money to Quintana. I think you have to think of it as a gift to yourself. You're giving yourself the comfort of saying that you trust her values. And if you don't trust her values, don't give it to her."

I said I did trust her values. I just didn't trust her common sense.

"Common sense is something people learn by doing. Not by having their parents do it for them."

3 January 2001

I said that after I talked to him last week I felt weirdly better. As of Wednesday night, nothing had changed or improved but it had finally come home to me that I could maintain a certain distance without abandoning her – that in any case my attempts to "solve" or manage Q's life were futile, that all I could do was try to live my own life. And then, beginning to some degree with her call on Thursday, she had seemed to be emerging from her free fall. The call on Thursday was still a little off in tone, but it seemed at least to indicate a recognition that she should be trying to manage her own life. I said I still didn't know whether she recognized this at a real level or was responding to what she thought our expectations were – but it was better than free fall.

I told him about the discussions you and I had had about friends, old and new – your saying that you had felt separated from our oldest friends, in the same way that I did. And about how – after dinner with the Halberstams and lunch on Saturday and seeing the Dickeys on Saturday night – we had both felt that we did have friends, they were just different friends.

"That's very positive," he said. "Especially for the two of you. You're limited in the resources you have within your own family. You have only the one child – no grandchildren – and that one child has only an up-and-down ability – more often than not down – to provide you with the minimum daily requirement of intimacy that you need. Intimacy is exactly what she has the most trouble handling. So you can't reliably get it from her. Which – for the two of you – makes it even more important than it is for most people to have close friends, to develop real intimacy outside the family. Losing friends – feeling apart from friends – is something that happens to most of us as we get older. Very few of us encourage new friendships. Most of us just retreat into our families. You can't. So the more you encourage friendship, the better off you'll be. You have to keep those connections alive. Entertaining is a big part of that. Again, as we get older, we tend to stop entertaining, it's just too much effort. You mentioned for example that you missed entertaining this Christmas."

I said that as much as I bitched about giving parties, it did make me feel useful in a way I didn't feel this Christmas.

"It's more than useful. It makes you feel connected. Connections are what you need most acutely."

I told him about the weddings of the Trillin girls, the second of which had for both of us been a kind of moment you couldn't just ignore or rationalize.

"That would be extremely traumatic," he said. "How many oldest friends do you have in your life? Then you find out – or you think you find out – that the friendship doesn't mean quite what you thought it did."

I said I didn't think it was Calvin. I thought it was just a case of acquiescing in what the girls wanted.

"That's what everybody does now. It's very unhealthy. It's not what a wedding should be about. Weddings aren't to make a star of the bride, they're to mark the moment when the couple together take their place in the community. That involves other people."

I told him about Q on New Year's Eve – maybe because we were in extremis too, it turned out to be a really close evening. She had come in and been a little weepy about everybody else going to a party and having a wonderful time – but it had been clear that in fact not everybody else was having a wonderful time, for example we weren't, and she had seemed to pick up on that. I said I had suggested to her – when she complained about AA that AA people didn't really reach out the way they said they did – that maybe she was not transmitting a willingness to accept help – that maybe she was a little like me, always trying to appear in charge, never wanting anyone to see me needing help because maybe they wouldn't give the help, maybe they'd reject me. And she had seemed to agree that she did this. Then, the next day when we talked to her, she seemed actually to have had a good time at the AA event – and when we commented on it, she said "you two made me feel better".

"That's what you've been working toward. That's the point you've been putting in all this work to get to. Her being able to say that. She still won't be able to express that closeness on a regular basis, but that she can express it at all is a big step forward."

I told him about my Livia Soprano conversation with Mother New Year's Day. She had "no idea" whether Jim was in town, but it later developed she had seen him that morning. "All he ever does is play golf," she had complained, but she had been after him for ten years to retire, and, after he did, to "stop flying around and play golf". Now he had "stopped flying around" and was playing golf, had in fact rented a house in Palm Desert and intended to do nothing but play golf for four months. Now this was the complaint. I said I realized that nothing he or I did or did not do could make her happy at this point, but I wondered if my brother realized it.

"I'd say if he's going to Palm Desert for four months, he realizes it."

17 January 2001

I told Dr. MacKinnon about dinner last night. Q saying she wanted to go to a noisy restaurant because she felt all she'd been doing was going to meetings and eating in diners. Then she said she had something to tell us, and told us her counselor at the Day Treatment Program wanted her to do this additional group, and she didn't like thinking she was "that sick". And I had said it wasn't a question of being sick, but why had the counselor recommended it? And she had said because she slipped last week and when they were talking about why she had slipped – "because I was lonely and depressed" – the counselor had suggested this additional program.

Then I told him about our conversation this morning. I recognized that I was always trying to step in and "solve her problem". I recognized that I had to stop this, and I was trying to, but sometimes it seemed as if she *expected* me to solve her problem, *wanted* me to. As if she had this extreme *passivity* about her own life.

"Of course she wants you to solve her problem," he said. "That's her deepest pattern. That's the basic source of her problem. Rather than thinking of it as an extreme passivity, however, you'd be closer to the mark if you thought of it as an extreme dependence. She is literally panicked by the idea of making a decision. She's afraid she'll make the wrong one."

I said I had talked to her on the phone today, and she said the counselor had said he would be glad to talk to me about the program. And I had said it wasn't about me, the decision wasn't up to me, it was up to her. And she would not accept this. At the end of the call she was still saying she would fax me the information and I could tell her what I thought.

"Did you say you wouldn't read it?"

Of course not, I said.

"Why not?"

I said that would seem as if I wasn't interested in her.

"Do you think there's the slightest doubt in her mind that you're interested in her?"

I said I supposed not.

"You're going to have to talk to her about this. She has this extreme dependence. You're the person she's dependent on, because you're the person she has turned to – all her life – to make her decisions. She's 34 now, and you're still stepping in. Of course she wants you to step in – because then it's your responsibility, not hers. You're giving her exactly what she wants: she can be free of responsibility and she can resent you for controlling her. That's her pattern. We haven't had much luck changing this pattern in her, so we're trying to change it in you. I think you should say to her – and you'll have to say it 25 or 100 times – 'I made a mistake. I let you become dependent on me. I thought that was how I could show you how much I loved you, I thought that was the way I could protect you, keep you safe. Now I know that I hurt you by overprotecting you. I'm sorry I didn't know it before. But now I'm going to change. I'm not going to make any more decisions for you. I can give you advice on how to make decisions – the process – ways to approach decisions – but I can't make them'."

I asked what advice on the process might be.

"Well, one thing she doesn't seem to realize is that not every decision is a life sentence. Take this program for example. She might think about trying it, see if it helps. This is short-term treatment. Nobody expects her to be in it for a long haul. If it helps, fine. If it doesn't, she'll know, she can make a new decision. But you can't. Tell her that unless she's in imminent danger – danger that you see and she doesn't – you're out of the decision business."

After a pause I said that I did in fact see an imminent danger. The danger I saw was that the more she thought of herself as an invalid – the more she isolated herself from a normal social life and a normal working life – the closer she was to suicide.

"I agree," he said. "However. She's not totally isolated in this program. It requires a good deal of social interaction. Which makes it better for her right now – in the short term – than sitting alone in her apartment drinking. Of course it has to feel like a step back – a retreat – to know that you were once a functioning member of a demanding work environment and now you're not. But she had reached a point at which she apparently couldn't function any more. And there are far worse situations she could be in right now than the day treatment program."

Still, I said . . .

"It's not real life," he said. "No. But it's not a permanent retreat. She'll return to real life. Once she's developed some skills for living a real life."

Then he returned to the question of suicide. "In a perverse way, what would keep her from suicide – maybe the single strong thing – is the idea that it would kill you and John. I've told you before, you have to keep this idea alive in her. As long as either of you is still alive, we don't think she'll go that far. And by the time you're gone, she will presumably have found something else worth living for."

We talked about suicide in general, Stephen's specifically. I said he had almost killed his children, like in the case a few weeks ago on Long Island.

"You know those cases where the mother kills herself and her children so as not to abandon them? We think there's some element of that in cases like the one on Long Island. Probably deeply unconscious, but a feeling that you can't abandon the family, you can't leave them alone and in pain."

31 January 2001

I discussed our sense of dinner at Dawat – that Q was OK, she was trying very hard, but ("or 'and' – I'm not sure what the right conjunction is here") she's not having any fun. We discussed this. I said that she was still clearly very depressed – you could see it in her inability to get simple things done, like getting a fax machine.

"Don't do it for her," he said. "Everything in you wants to make it easier for her, but if you do it for her you deprive her of the satisfaction of having done it herself. This kind of inability to perform mundane tasks is entirely typical of depression. It's obviously something they work on in her group sessions."

I said it was, she had said so. So she was trying. Still, she wasn't getting things done – and this kind of organization had been second nature to her at age 16, 17 – I had been in awe of it, because I myself tended to procrastinate, get involved in doing one thing and let everything else slide. She had never been that way.

"Her ability or inability to get these simple things done is the most obvious gauge of her depression. She has to work it through herself. That's what she's doing in her current situation."

I said I had heard, last night and before last night, something worrying in her attitude to her current situation. "Contempt" would be too strong a word, I said, but there was something.

"Self-deprecation?" he suggested.

Not strong enough, I said. I couldn't quite put my finger on it.

"It has to be very difficult for her," he said. "One day she's a contributing member of society, she has a good job, she has a salary, she has an office, she has a title, then the next day she has none of those things. She's on her own."

I said it was a little more than just being on her own. She wasn't thinking of herself as "on her own". She seemed to be thinking of herself as a patient.

"And there's an element of shame," he suggested. "She loathes the situation she's in, and she to some extent loathes herself for being in it."

Yes, I said. That was the hint I got. And I didn't know to what extent I could talk to her about it.

"I don't think you can, unless she brings it up. Unless she at least alludes to it."

I said she had alluded to it last night, but I hadn't known how to pick it up. She had seen someone she thought she knew in the restaurant, and had said something in passing about not knowing what to say when people asked what she was doing. "What am I supposed to say, I'm in this outpatient loony bin?" And neither of us had picked it up.

"When she alludes to it that way, I think the thing to stress is how much strength it shows that she can do this – that she can put her life or her career on hold while she works to get healthy – that requires more strength than most people have. Emphasize the strength. The long-term benefit. The thing to avoid is seeming to confirm – by your silence or even by your acquiescence – what she can't help thinking you think, and what she herself most fears – that she's doing nothing."

7 February 2001

I brought up the piece in Sunday's LAT about the 10 year old who was killed in the course of unlicensed therapy for reactive attachment disorder. I said the piece had made me think about a lot of things – (1) whether the child was truly disordered or whether the mother had simply needed more affection than any child (let alone this child) was able to give; (2) whether this was part of the dynamic in the troubled Eastern European adoptions; (3) whether this was to a perhaps lesser extent true of all adoptive parents, at least mothers – i.e., don't they by definition need a child in a stronger than perhaps normal way?

"I would say that to one extent or another it is true, yes. I did have a patient, by the way, who adopted a Russian child. The child had been adopted in Russia, then given back, then adopted a second time and given back. So by the time this five-year-old arrived in this country – speaking not a word of English – she was a deeply troubled child."

He said that a few years ago he had sat at a P&S alumni dinner next to a woman, the president of the alumni association, who specialized in attachment disorders and claimed to be having considerable success with an alternative therapy. "She rents a gym for 3 days, she gets 3 generations of the family into the gym, everybody sits on mats and tells everybody else what they expected and how they were disappointed. Et cetera. Lots of hugging, but none of the stuff that was going on in the case you described. She claims to be successfully treating attachment disorders even in adults. She also claims to be successfully treating autism, so I'm not entirely unskeptical. The older I get, however – and I've noticed this among my colleagues – the more willing I am to entertain alternative medicine. You can't not. When you see the shortcomings of traditional medicine. Particularly in my field. I did refer the patient with the Russian child to her."

I said that thinking about the piece had made me think I had from the beginning needed too much of Quintana. That she was bearing this burden.

"Isn't that what we've been talking about? But don't take all the blame on yourself, she's a very difficult patient, a very hard case."

I said I recognized that. Something else that this piece brought up: I recognized in the description of attachment disorder a pattern that she has. A way of seeming charming and perfect to the world at large even when she's falling apart. A way of dissembling, even lying, not least to herself. I said if you read the alcoholism literature this pattern is attributed to the alcohol. She herself, picking up on the literature, describes it as "typical alcoholic behavior." But seeing it described as an attachment disorder made me wonder if in fact it began with the alcohol.

"It's not the alcohol. It's the personality. The alcohol comes into play as a way of medicating the personality disorder."

I said that this skill at dissembling made it very hard for us to gauge at any given time how she was. Right now, for example, she seemed a little more even. She was more involved with AA. She had mentioned the last time we saw her that she was waiting to make an insurance decision about her business until she had a clearer idea what she was going to be doing – that Dr. Kass had told her she could cut back on her group sessions if she found something worthwhile to do, and she was thinking of doing some computer training.

"That sounds very good, but as you know, she has a deep investment in making herself sound good to you. By the way, I hope you realize – when you describe the charm and the skill at dissembling that characterize attachment disorders – that the most significant American on the landscape for the past eight years is a walking attachment disorder."

I said I assumed he meant Clinton.

"Textbook. The need to win over, to charm. The anger, the self-pity. He doesn't attach, he seduces."

I said he did seem to have one true attachment, to Chelsea.

"Absolutely. Which is going to be hard on her. Nothing about families turns out to be easy, does it."

Speaking of families: I said that these thoughts provoked by the piece had made me realize that the appearance of Quintana's "other family" had been for us a good deal more traumatic than we could at the time afford to consider. At the time it happened, Quintana's deep upset was our main focus, and our every instinct was to try to "normalize" the situation. When we met Erin* for example we treated it as a normal "social" situation, as if it was just another dinner in a restaurant with a new cute friend of Quintana's. There was no other way to deal with it, and yet it kept me from facing exactly what I thought about it. Everything about the appearance of this family, I could say now, was like the bottom falling out, a threat, and not just to Quintana. At some level I never admitted I feared who she would pick. I was afraid if they fought for her and we graciously didn't, we'd lose by default.

"I think this exacerbated depression that eventually brought you to see me actually started then. It tells me something that you've never before now discussed it except in terms of its effect on Quintana. When, really, I'm incapable of imagining a worse intrusion on your particular life."

* The biological sister who got in touch with Quintana.

4 April 2001

I said I had just come from a lunch, and had found myself unable to remember anything the speaker said long enough to write it down.

"Did this upset you," he asked.

I said yes. I said that I was more and more aware of this, that you were too, that we had talked about it, that both of us had trouble thinking of words or maintaining a thought long enough to follow it through, that I had said to you that it was emotional overload, stress, and to some extent I supposed it was but it was worrisome. For example I couldn't remember a phone number long enough to dial it.

"So you write it down, and you still have to glance at it to finish dialing?"

Yes, I said.

"Welcome to the club," he said. "But let's get back to this lunch. Was what the speaker was saying important to you?"

In fact no, I said. I had already written whatever I was going to write about the subject, there was no reason for me to even be there except to please Bob Silvers.* Still, taking notes was what I did, and on this occasion I couldn't seem to do it.

"I would suspect there was a dissonance between what was being said and what was actually on your mind."

In this case possibly, I said. But it also seemed to be a breakdown of short-term memory.

"There are tricks for getting around that. They're the same tricks you use when you're learning to study, to read for an exam. You hear it or read it, then you repeat it to yourself – 2 or 3 times if it's

* Robert Silvers was the editor of *The New York Review of Books* from 1963 until his death in 2017.

really important – then you write it down. The reason for this is that hearing or reading gets laid down in one part of your brain, speaking it in another, and writing it down in still a third. So if you've got cell loss in one part, you've still got it laid down in the other two. Telling someone else also works. Not because you expect them to remember it and remind you. Just because you've reinforced it in your own mind. My schedule is so limited and so much the same every week that I often don't even look at my calendar. So if there's something out of the ordinary coming up – say a changed appointment – I'll often ask the patient to call and remind me. Whether the patient calls or not, I will then remember. Because I've reinforced it to myself by talking about it."

He picked up a stack of notes by his telephone. "See these? They're things I might need to remember. They're here so I know where they are. It's not just age. I see my son write everything down on his Palm Pilot, and he's only in his 40s. As far as things like telephone numbers go, you can't remember them because they aren't important to you. If I gave you a seven digit number right now and told you it was crucial that you remember it, you would remember it, you'd devise a trick for remembering it. The telephone number isn't up front in your mind. Your mind at that moment is on the call, what you're going to say when the other person answers. Anybody's mind."

I said I often thought it would help just to have a week free. To not be under any pressure, to get the house put in order, all the pieces of paper put in place.

"That would be very valuable. In fact it's another trick. Straightening out your office or your house actually reorders your mind. It has a measurable physiological effect, it's been documented. I myself have been cleaning out my files, because I ran out of filing space, I could no longer afford to keep 50 years of tax records. It's time-consuming, but it's been extremely useful."

I told him about the dumpster when we left California. That it felt liberating, but also traumatic. That I thought even now about things I had thrown out. That there was no reason in the world I needed to know for example how much it cost to take Quintana to the Royal Hawaiian in 1969 but I acutely missed not being able to look it up.

"There's no reason I need to have checks my mother wrote when I was a child," he said. "But until now I kept them. I couldn't throw them out. They were somehow pieces of a life."

On the subject of mothers, I said that mine seemed better most of the time but then would let slip something deluded. For instance she remained unconvinced that she had not had a lung removed in the hospital. When I tried to correct this, she said "I know what they did, I saw the bill." I said I supposed I should call her doctor about this.

"Just so he knows what's going on, yes."

I said I had been thinking about something he said last week. He had said that trying to intervene on behalf of my mother might well be in vain, but that it was still important that I do it, because to not do it would be inconsistent with my image of myself as a caring person.

"Exactly."

Well, I said, I'm not at all sure that "a caring person" is in fact my image of myself.

"Is that what was on your mind at lunch? How you were going to have to walk in here and tell me this truth I had somehow failed to recognize? Come clean about having put one over on me? Masquerading as a caring person when you're not? Why exactly do you think you're not a caring person?"

I said it had just never been my image of myself. It was tied up with my working, leaving home, the selfishness it took to . . .

"Do productive work?" he interrupted.

I said it did take a certain selfishness. A certain self-focus. Which lately I had been hard put to summon up.

"In our culture this is something not many girls escape. Some deep idea that they should be the caring ones, the ones to stay home, the ones to take care of ill family members. You rejected that, but you didn't escape feeling guilty about it. This affects more women than men, but men don't get off as free as some women think they do."

I asked if he knew, when he said what he said last week about my image of myself as a caring person, that this wasn't my image of myself.

"I can't say I'm entirely surprised. I did think you might have developed more self-awareness. But you really don't see yourself as other people see you, do you? Other people – myself included – see you as extremely caring. On the other hand, if you saw yourself that way, you wouldn't be here. Which is where we're trying to get."

3 July 2001

Some chat about Honolulu, how long we had been going there.
I explained about going out from California whenever we (and
especially me after MS diagnosis)* got tired. That Quintana had
been there a lot. I had taught her the multiplication tables there. I
had gotten her through "Moby Dick" there.

"What just made you sad," he asked.

I said it was nothing really.

"It was a thought. A thought isn't nothing."

I said I guessed it was the memory of how bright and happy she
had seemed then, as opposed to how she had been these past few
years. I said it surprised me that this opposition occurred to me
now, because I thought I had resolved it in Honolulu.

"Parents don't easily resolve their feelings about seeing a child go
through pain."

I said I had taken out a piece I had torn from a paper. The piece
had troubled me when I first read it here. It was about American
businesses taking a new hard line on hiring people with any
hint of alcoholism. It was driving their insurance up, it was seen
as costing too much. It had occurred to me when I read it that
Quintana had become for many businesses unhireable. Then,
when I read the piece again after several days in Honolulu, I had
seen it more evenly: the history of everybody's 20s and 30s, after
all, is one of the awareness of doors closing. At one age – very
young – it occurs to you that you'll never be a ballet dancer. At a
later age you think you'll never be this, never be that. You make
your life around what you have left, what doors haven't closed.
This happens to everybody. What happened to Q wasn't really
that different. So, I said, I thought I was on top of this.

* Didion was tentatively diagnosed with multiple sclerosis when she was in her
thirties, although the symptoms did not recur.

"Actually, given the anti-discrimination laws, no prospective employer could ever find out her history. They may want to know, but they can't ask. They can't afford to have her volunteer it. When I was interviewing for the medical school, I was warned never to ask any question that might elicit that kind of answer. Say there was a missing year on a c.v., I couldn't even ask what the applicant had done that year. Even with a trained psychiatrist doing the interviewing – me – people did slip through. We had a suicide, and learned after the fact that it had followed any number of attempts that we hadn't known about. Any overt hint of a problem that did slip into the interview would make us more inclined to hire, to avoid potential suits. So your specific fears were in this case groundless. That doesn't stop the emotion that prompted those fears from being real."

I said I had picked up a book in Honolulu on AA. By one of the anti-AA recovery people. Not one of the "moderation" people, one of the Rational Recovery type people who thought abstinence could be better achieved outside AA, mainly because AA both isolated the alcoholic from everything that wasn't AA and made the alcoholic see him or herself as perpetually sick, the "slip" being guaranteed. I said that my feelings about AA were at the moment necessarily quite mixed – I agreed fervently with many things in this book – yet Quintana had for some months been doing well with AA, or at least with something. I just wished that it weren't so isolating.

"I agree with you. It can be isolating for some people. Some people seem to need that. It takes them away from everything else, then it fills their life with AA."

I said this was what seemed to me the setup in the program. If you get to a point where you define your entire life as "not drinking", you're defining yourself – whether you "slip" or don't – as "sick", or "defective". Every meeting you go to confirms this message.

"I agree. It can be dangerous. But I think Quintana has been showing common sense about it."

I said that at least she had seemed not to buy into her sponsor's suggestion that she drop therapy, on the grounds that "AA is a fulltime job". I told him about her sponsor also suggesting that it wasn't wise for her to go through her grandmother's things with me on July 4, on the grounds that holidays were dangerous and she should be with AA people. I said I knew holidays were dangerous, that's why I had suggested we do it.

"Good idea. Especially since Dr. Kass is away this week. I have the impression she's fairly reliant on him in this period." [As I write this I remember how he was able to point out "feet as metaphor" to her – and make her get it – whereas if we had said it, it would have sent her spiraling.]

We talked then about my brother, and his curious reaction to Mother's death. The trip to Oregon, the pictures, etc. I said that he had always more or less dismissed her. Not out of hostility – it was just part of the culture in which he grew up.

"It sounds as if he's reached a point where he's looking at his own mortality. Family deaths do that. You don't see that many generations ahead of you, so you start making connections with those behind you."

I said these connections had always been a big thing in our family. Jim had ignored all that, but I had it ingrained in me. Then when Quintana was born I just dropped it. It lost all meaning for me.

"You didn't see a branch for her on your family tree? She wasn't blood?"

I said it wasn't that. It was that my attachment to her was so strong that blood lost its meaning for me.

"I suspect this probably reflected your own feeling – going back to earliest childhood – that you were different, not part of the family."

I said if he was going to tell me again that every sensitive child imagined himself to be adopted, forget it, because I never ever imagined I was adopted.

"Adoption is just a metaphor here. You don't have to literally believe yourself adopted to feel not part of a family. Many people feel at some point that other parents might have loved them more, appreciated them more. There's a deep reason for the persistence of the changeling myth. Every little child is surrounded by family members pointing out his or her resemblance to this side or that side of the family. Her mother's eyes, her father's temper, all that. No child can hear that and not wonder at some level, well, what if I didn't look like them? Would they still keep me?"

I said that one of the most troubling things to Quintana, when she went to Dallas, was people saying she looked like this side or that side.

"That would have been devastating to her. Because her whole family structure was you and John and your families. She and you had an equal investment in her 'looking like you' – at whatever level you defined that. What they said to her in Dallas was understandable, but nothing they could say would have upset her more."

Let's say you were adopted, I said. Say you're Quintana. Go back to this thing of children wondering if other parents might have loved them more, appreciated them more. You would think that someone adopted would think that of her natural parents, but to the best of my knowledge Quintana never did.

"Of course she didn't. They gave her away. Do you think that was lost on her?"

Which would mean, I said, that when she got mad at us, she would hit a wall. She couldn't afford to get mad at us. Because in her mind she might lose us.

"That's a dilemma that's heightened for adopted children, yes. But it's not unshared by the rest of us. There's an ambivalence in every intense relationship. The ambivalence is what makes the relationship intense. You love, you hate. Growing up is a process of learning to accept that ambivalence."

26 December 2001

I told Dr. MacKinnon about Q's saying last night, when I asked how she was doing in terms of money, that she was "all right until April, well, May, when my money from Paine Webber stops, so some adjustment will have to be made then."

"Adjustment by whom?" he asked.

I said we didn't get into it, just said that we would have to discuss that.

"The adjustment that needs to be made is, she gets a job."

I said that obviously, this was our feeling. I said that I had been thinking about it and I thought the best approach was to just assume that this was in fact the "adjustment" she had in mind, and to open by discussing what kind of job she had in mind.

"What has she been living on?"

I said that at Christmas a year ago she was given $100,000 by us and $10,000 by her grandmother, giving her $110,000 tax free. If this will run out in April she has been receiving and spending $6,800 a month tax free, which is considerably more than double what she was making after tax when she was working. Plus, we have been paying for her medical bills and her homeowners insurance, so she has had few major expenses.

"The idea, of course, was that it was an investment in her future, a backup while she got started on her own work, but she apparently didn't see it that way. There's a message in that. The message is that giving her further money is a disincentive to her learning how to take care of herself. I think you need to discuss this with her at the earliest possible opportunity, because she needs to start looking for a job. I know that you yourself have been concerned about money and the future – what sentient person at this moment isn't concerned about money and the future – but your own concerns have nothing to do with this conversation with her. Giving her the idea that you're cutting her off because you don't have the money would be digging yourself a guilt hole you'll never climb out of. The idea to convey isn't that you don't have the money. The idea is that she needs to progress in her own life, and that you've come to the conclusion that continuing to support her is keeping her from making this progress. You can continue to help her in a limited way, say by paying her medical bills, her insurance, whatever. But it's clearly not helping her to keep her on the dole. What does she think most people in New York do between jobs? Actors work as waiters. Kids writing novels work as temps. Everybody finds ways of making a living to support what they really want to do. Quintana should certainly appreciate that. She knows that you and John write movies to support your other work."

I said she didn't seem to get it.

"The time has come for reality to confront her. Since she seems unable to confront it herself. I think this would be a useful discussion to have in a joint session with Dr. Kass."

I said I presumed he meant after discussing it with Quintana.

"Actually I meant to have the conversation with Quintana and Dr. Kass at the same time. My guess is that Dr. Kass has been looking for a way to motivate her, and has been running into the wall of her not needing the money because she's being supported."

I said I thought to have such a conversation would be to mousetrap her.

"That's because you think of cutting off the money as punishment. It's not punishment. It's what she needs to grow. It's got everything to do with what Dr. Kass is trying to do. It's not a conversation about not supporting her financially. It's a conversation about supporting her emotionally. I think you could very easily suggest to Quintana that you and she discuss this with Dr. Kass. Think about it."

3 January 2002

Discussion of Zoloft. Raise to one tablet. Discussion of swallowing, pills and in general. I said I had noticed difficulty swallowing, that I found myself choking.

"As you get older those muscles don't work as automatically. It's like balance, you have to fight it, retrain the muscles. It's essential to fight these things, to be aware of where you are developing weaknesses and overcome them. If for the next three months you try to become aware of chewing and swallowing, I think you'll notice a significant difference."

I said that we had initiated discussion with Q of her plans. I said that it had gone generally well, but there had been one shaky place, where she had gone negative over the question of the book and the computer equipment and what you do first.

"I hope you pointed out that you have to take it one step at a time, and that with every step you take you gain confidence for the next step. You can't think in terms of the whole thing you have to do, you can't try to achieve it all at once, you'd just throw up your hands and throw in the towel."

I said that we had tried to stress the step by step process. We discussed Hawaii. I said we had conveyed the idea that she would have to support herself. I said that she had said she wanted to make her life more simple, that she could for example "work in the pineapple fields," but that she seemed to lack any clear idea of what she would or could do.

"Obviously, what's driving this Hawaii move at the moment is the idea of just getting away. Getting away from you, getting away from Dr. Kass, starting over. Going west, if you will."

I said that going west traditionally entailed some expectation that there would be hardships involved.

"I think that's the import of saying she could pick pineapples. That's what she's saying, that she's willing to do it."

I said I thought what was driving it was the idea that she could get away from thinking of herself as a sick person. Obviously, given her history over the past few years – the rehab, the multiple hospitalizations – she sees herself as visibly damaged. She wants to go somewhere where no one will automatically look at her and see the same thing. Where no one will automatically say "How are you doing, how's it going." I said I thought she had to be sick of that. That in fact it had come up every time she hit bottom. "Why do I have to be this sick person," in many variations.

"Then that's very healthy. I would be very encouraged if that was her motivation."

I said she had been thinking of going out for 2 weeks, to try to find a job and a place to live, but we weren't sure that was long enough.

"Definitely it's not long enough. Tell her to give herself enough time."

I said we had thought maybe three months.

"That's much more in the right time frame, yes."

I said she was confused about what to do with her apartment here, and we had said do nothing for the time being.

"Exactly. Nothing. She needs someplace to come back to if this turns out to be not what she wants."

I said I wondered if we should suggest – if she wanted to wait until late May or June – that we go out with her and see that she gets settled.

"Absolutely the wrong idea. If she can't do this on her own, she shouldn't do it. If she's going to gain the confidence she needs, she needs to do it herself."

What, I said, if she can't do it.

"Then she can't. You can't control or affect that. The only message you have to convey is that it wouldn't be the end of the world. It's an adventure. Let her try it. Don't expect the worst, don't treat her like a sick person."*

* This is the last known detailed account of Didion's sessions with MacKinnon, although she saw him at least until early 2012, at which point he was getting old (eighty-five). He retired from private practice in 2014 and died in 2017. His obituary in *The New York Times* noted that he was "one of the most skilled clinicians of his era." He was known as an old-fashioned Freudian, a staunch defender of talk therapy. An article in *The New York Times Magazine* in December 1992 titled "Off the Couch," which discusses his disdain for chemical therapeutics, refers to him as "John Wayne in a blue suit."

JAN 9 03 DR. KASS*

Q was a few minutes late. Dr. Kass asked me to come in. I asked if he wanted to begin without Q. He said it was up to me, then said no, you're right, it would make her paranoid.

A minute or so later Q came in, emitting waves of negative attitude. "Didn't he come out," she demanded. I said we were waiting for her. She brushed past me into the office and sat down. I followed and sat down.

I said I didn't know how aware he was of the precipitating incident. Quintana interrupted and said he wasn't aware, she hadn't been able to get an appt until today. Then why don't you tell him about it, I said. She told him that she had seen Dr. Roscan and told him that she didn't see any point in continuing to see him since she was still drinking "from time to time." End of story from her.

I said that there was a further aspect to my being there, and explained about our January 30 encounter.

Dr. Kass said that Dr. Roscan had in fact called him. During the course of this it became clear that it was Dr. Roscan rather than Q, as we assumed, who had terminated treatment. Dr. Roscan had told him that he didn't know what would help Quintana at this point, but he had become convinced that any conventional program – up to and including the standard 28-day rehab – would be ineffective. The missing element being that she was not making the decision to stop drinking. The only thing he could think of – and he could offer no assurance that it would work – was a much longer treatment. He had mentioned to Dr. Kass a place in Pennsylvania called Alima Lodge. Quintana allowed that he had also mentioned this to her. Dr. Kass was unfamiliar with it.

* Didion's description of the visit with Quintana's psychiatrist was not among the papers found in the file next to her desk. It was in her computer.

Dr. Kass had concluded, after talking to Dr. Roscan, that he himself should also suspend treatment. He could not continue to prescribe medication for her knowing how much she was drinking. It was too dangerous, the risk of interaction with alcohol outweighed any possible benefit.

He said there had been a period when she seemed to be on an upswing – controlling this to some extent, taking a few steps toward putting her life back together. That period had ended.

At this point she started talking about how hard the holidays had been ("I'm not making excuses"), everything in her life was going down around her, her father was sick, her love life was going down, her career was going down.

I said this was depression talking, her father was handling his health, her career had just reached a point where – if she wanted to – she could restart it.

Dr. Kass said that this down period – this period of heavy drinking – long preceded the holidays. "You've been drinking today," he said, "and heavily." And in fact it was clear that she had. At this point she cried.

Let's talk about this, Dr. Kass said. Let's talk about the idea that a radical change of scene would help you. You're always talking about moving to Hawaii. I don't think that would help you – but tell me why you think it would.

Familiar drunk ramble about how much she hates New York, about how everybody is always on her back, asking her questions, her mother is always asking her questions and talking about money etc etc.

I said I didn't know where this hostility was coming from, I wasn't asking her any questions, I was trying to keep her alive. Because she was killing herself day by day.

You and I agree on that, Dr. Kass said. Not only is she killing herself day by day, but she can't make any life in whatever time she has left – the alcohol keeps her from carrying through on plans, from maintaining relationships, from everything that makes a life.

I said I had told her that I couldn't stand by and watch her do that. Because it would kill me as well.

Dr. Kass said he didn't think that was a helpful thing to lay on her. You and I had done our job when she was small, and done it fairly well, not perfectly but well. You can't save her life now. Only she can do that. It's not useful to lay it on her that she has to live to keep you alive. I refrained from saying that Dr. MacKinnon had told me to lay it on her every chance I got because in his experience it was the only thing that prevented suicide.

Some discussion of show in May. Dr. Kass said it would be too bad if she were to go into some kind of longterm treatment that would prevent her from doing the show. I said she was going to have to stop drinking before she went to California. For one thing she would be driving, and she could kill herself or someone else by driving drunk. For another thing she would be staying with friends, and she couldn't be drunk in other people's lives.

At which point she became very angry and said of course she would stop drinking before she went to California, end of conversation, there's nothing else to say, what are we doing here saying the same thing over and over.

At this impasse I asked Dr. Kass if he knew Marc Galanter. He said yes, absolutely, he was one of the few people he respected in the substance abuse field, it was a name he had often thought of mentioning. Marc Galanter had in fact trained him at one point. He thought a consult with Dr. Galanter could be a logical first step here. Did Quintana want him to make the call? Quintana said yes. Dr. Kass called his office and asked them to reach

Dr. Galanter and have him call, he wanted to refer a patient as soon as possible.

Dr. Kass will see Q again on Thursday Jan 23 at 12:30. The idea is that by then she will have seen Dr. Galanter. A plan will be discussed at that point.

On July 26, 2003, a little more than six months after Didion sat with Quintana in the psychiatrist's office, Quintana was married. She and her husband lived in her old apartment, not far from the Didion/Dunne apartment. On December 22, Quintana was not feeling well, and her husband took her to a nearby hospital then known as Beth Israel North. She was diagnosed with the flu and sent home. On December 25, her husband took her back to the hospital. She was diagnosed with pneumonia, admitted to the ICU, and intubated. The next day, she was in septic shock. John Gregory Dunne had a heart attack and died on December 30.

On January 22, 2004, Quintana was discharged from Beth Israel North and three days later was admitted to New York–Presbyterian Hospital with pulmonary emboli. She was released after a week and was able to attend her father's funeral on March 23. She and her husband flew to Los Angeles for a vacation on March 25. She fell at the airport and was taken to the UCLA Medical Center, where she had surgery for a subdural hematoma.

Late in April 2004, Quintana was moved from the acute neuro-rehabilitation unit at the UCLA Medical Center and brought to New York, where she was treated at the Rusk Institute at New York University Medical Center for two and a half months. After she was discharged from Rusk, she received outpatient therapy.

Quintana was admitted to the ICU at New York Weill Cornell Medical Center with acute pancreatitis on June 14, 2005. On

August 3, surgery revealed a necrotic colon and peritonitis. She died on August 26. She was thirty-nine.

One of the doctors who had treated Quintana for substance abuse wrote to Didion after Quintana died. In a letter found in her computer, Didion replied gratefully and told him that during the last hospitalization, Quintana had said she would like to get back into therapy. She speculated on what had in the end caused her daughter's death.

"I still have trouble sorting out how much of what happened to her was alcoholism and how much depression and how much an only marginally connected cascade of disastrous medical events," she wrote. "I recognize the connection of pancreatitis to alcoholism but I am not sure she would have had pancreatitis had there not been 18 prior months of illness, from the original septic shock to the pulmonary emboli that followed to the bleed into the brain that ensued from the coumadin for the emboli."

A NOTE ON THE TYPE

This book was set in Times New Roman, the font that Joan Didion used on her computer when she typed the notes to John.

Composed by North Market Street Graphics,
Lancaster, Pennsylvania